# Learn JavaScript

## Chuck Easttom

**Wordware Publishing, Inc.**

**Library of Congress Cataloging-in-Publication Data**

Easttom, Chuck.
   Learn JavaScript / by Chuck Easttom.
     p.  cm.
   Includes index.
   ISBN 1-55622-856-2 (pbk.)
   1. JavaScript (Computer program language).  I. Title.
   QA76.73.J39 E38    2001
   005.2'762--dc21

2001046844
CIP

© 2002, Wordware Publishing, Inc.

All Rights Reserved

2320 Los Rios Boulevard
Plano, Texas 75074

Printed in the United States of America

ISBN 1-55622-856-2
10 9 8 7 6 5 4 3 2 1
0110

All inquiries for volume purchases of this book should be addressed to Wordware Publishing, Inc., at the above address. Telephone inquiries may be made by calling:

(972) 423-0090

# Contents Summary

# Contents

**v**

# Acknowledgments

Writing a book is a very difficult task, and it is never the work of a single person. I would like to take the time to thank some of the people who were indispensable in making this book happen:

Jim Hill and Wes Beckwith, the wonderful guys at Wordware Publishing who labored through this with me. Without Jim and Wes, this book simply could not have happened. Their ideas and input helped create this book. Not to mention that Jim always paid for lunch!

A very special thanks to Norman Smith who did an outstanding technical review of this book. Norm, you saved me from really embarrassing myself. Your review work is simply top notch.

Finally, I need to thank my wife, Misty, and my son, AJ, who both tolerated me spending hours secluded in my den working on this project. Without all of these people, this book would never have happened.

# Introduction

## Prerequisites

This book assumes you have absolutely no prior knowledge of JavaScript. A basic working knowledge of HTML is preferred but not essential. The first two chapters provide a basic introduction on HTML and JavaScript. The rest of the book takes you step by step through the process of building an actual web site using both HTML and JavaScript. However, the main emphasis of this book is teaching you JavaScript. After Chapter 1, "HTML Primer," all HTML is simply shown to provide context for the JavaScript, and an explanation for the HTML code is not usually given. However, only standard HTML techniques are used and the code is presented in a very organized manner so that anyone with a basic knowledge of HTML can easily follow along.

As each new concept is introduced, I will first explain the concept in a generic context and then I will show how it applies specifically to the web site we are building. In this way, you will get both the concept and the application.

## How to Read This Book

Some computer programming books are meant for you to simply take what you need from certain chapters. This book is intended for you to read from start to finish. If you follow the examples provided, when you complete the book you will have a completely functional web site with lots of HTML and plenty of interesting JavaScripts.

## Programming Style

As both an aid to the reader and to illustrate good programming practices, I use a uniform style throughout this entire text and in all the sample code, which you can download from www.wordware.com/javascript. I also have a tendency to comment very heavily—some would say too much. This comes from teaching and creating code samples for students. I hope you will find this helpful:

```
for (var intcounter = 0; intcounter < 10; ++intcounter)
{
   [JavaScript statements]
}// end of for loop
```

Some JavaScript scripters prefer to use a different style:

```
for (var num = 0; num < 10; ++num){
   [JavaScript statements]
}
```

A lot of my style preferences are just that, preferences. It is hard to call one style right and another wrong. However, I strongly suggest when you are writing code to consider the fact that other programmers will probably need to read your code at some point. You don't want them to have absolutely no idea what you were thinking when you wrote your code. I try to write code in such a way that even a novice programmer with no prior knowledge of the project at hand could easily deduce the intended purpose of the code.

 **NOTE:** Many tags in HTML <u>must</u> be closed. The <B> tag must be closed with </B>. However some tags, such as <TD> and <TR>, do not have to be closed. Some HTML programmers prefer to close them anyway. I do not. This is simply a style difference, but one you will see throughout this book.

## Special Features

Each chapter takes you step by step through several examples showing the techniques that chapter focuses on. The end of each chapter has a section called Antique Bookstore Project. As you read through the book, this section will gradually build a complete web site for a fictitious antique bookstore. It is my hope that this will give you a good feel for the process of developing a commercial web site. All the code for the finished web site can be downloaded from www.wordware.com/javascript.

## The Code

The code for this book can be downloaded from www.wordware.com/javascript. All the chapter examples are there ready to run. Note that the numbered examples in the text correspond to the examples in the code files. The complete Antique Bookstore Project is also included. Finally, there is a folder full of extra samples you can use in your own web sites. I strongly recommend you browse the code and use the resources provided for you.

# Chapter 1

# HTML Primer

This chapter is provided to give you a basic working knowledge of HTML. For those readers who lack this knowledge or feel that they may need a refresher, this chapter is essential to following the rest of the book. Experienced HTML programmers, however, should feel free to skip this chapter. JavaScript is a scripting language that is embedded into HTML documents in order to add significant functionality to those web pages. For this reason a working knowledge of HTML is essential to understanding and using JavaScript. I will be introducing some interesting HTML tags as we go through the book; however, I feel that getting you up to speed with a basic knowledge is critical.

HTML, or Hypertext Markup Language, is a relatively simple markup language that web browsers can use to display web pages. You can write HTML code in any text editor. I personally use Windows Notepad. Just remember when you save the file to save it as an .htm or .html file. The browser recognizes files with the .htm and .html extensions and will look in them for valid HTML code. HTML has had a long history and has gone through a number of revisions. Each successive revision adds more functionality to HTML, and with the current version (as of this writing) of HTML (Version 4.0), it is a very powerful language that can take some time to learn. Fortunately, most work on web pages can be done with just the essentials of HTML, and that is what this chapter will teach you.

 **NOTE:** Many tags in HTML <u>must</u> be closed. For example, the <B> tag must be closed with </B>. However, some tags, such as <TD> and <TR>, do not have to be closed. Some HTML programmers prefer to close them anyway. I do not. This is simply a style difference, but one you will see throughout this book.

The first question is how do we get the web browser to know that our document has HTML codes for it to read? HTML code is composed of *tags* that let the browser know what is to be done with certain text. At the beginning of your document you place the command <HTML> and at the end you put </HTML>; the web browser will know that the codes in between are supposed to be HTML.

```
<HTML>
    put HTML code here
</HTML>
```

You have to admit that this is pretty simple. But this web page won't do much of anything at all. So let's do the obligatory "Hello World" sample that every programming book starts off with. It will show you how to do text and some basic HTML.

**Example 1-1**

```
<HTML>
<HEAD>
    <TITLE>My First HTML Page</TITLE>
</HEAD>
<BODY>
<P><CENTER>
<B><FONT SIZE="+2">Hello World</FONT></B>
</CENTER>
</BODY>
</HTML>
```

Believe it or not this little snippet shows you most of what you need to know about HTML. To begin with, note that everything is contained between the <HTML> and </HTML> tags. These two commands define the beginning and the end of the HTML document. The web browser will ignore any items outside these commands. Next we have a section that is contained between the <HEAD> and </HEAD> commands. This is the header portion of your HTML document. The <TITLE> and </TITLE> commands contain the title that will actually appear in the title bar of your browser. A lot more can be done in the head section, but that will be addressed as we work our way through this book.

Then we have the <BODY> and </BODY> commands. As you might have guessed this is the body of your HTML document. This is where most of your web page's code is going to go. Now inside the body section we have some text and some additional text that defines how the text will appear in the browser. The <P> command defines the beginning and the end of a paragraph. The <B> and </B> commands tell the browser to make whatever text is between them bold. <FONT SIZE="+2"> tells the browser how big the text should be (there are a variety of methods for doing this, as we shall see). The </FONT> command ends the font section of the HTML code. If you entered the HTML code correctly, then you should be able to view your web page in any browser and see an image much like that in Figure 1-1.

Figure 1-1

By now I trust you have noticed a pattern. All the commands have an opening command and a closing command. Well, this is true for all but a very few HTML commands. Just remember this rule: You close the commands in opposite order of how you opened them. Notice in Example 1-1 I opened the commands before the text like this: <P><CENTER><B><FONT SIZE="+2">, and then closed them like this: </FONT></B></CENTER>. (<P> does not need to be closed.) This is important to remember. You can think of this as "backing out" of your commands.

## Images and Hyperlinks

What we have so far gives you a very simple web page that displays one phrase in bold text. Admittedly, this is not very impressive, but if you understand the concepts involved with using these HTML commands then you conceptually understand HTML. Now let's expand your knowledge of HTML. Usually web pages contain more than simply a title and some text. Other items you might put in a web page would include images and links to other web pages. Placing an image on an HTML document is rather simple:

```
<IMG SRC="imagepath\imagename" WIDTH=52 HEIGHT=88 ALIGN=bottom>
```

You simply provide the path to the image and the name of the image, including its file extension (such as .gif, .bmp, .jpg, etc.). The other properties in this command allow you to alter the placement and size of the image. You can alter its width and height as well as its alignment.

You will also note that when you first place an image on an HTML page it has a border around it. You can get rid of this by adding BORDER = 0 into the tag, as in this example:

```
<IMG SRC="somepic.gif" BORDER =0>
```

Putting a hyperlink to another web site or to an e-mail address is just as simple:

```
<A HREF="http://www.wordware.com">
```

This link will connect to the URL (uniform resource locator) contained inside the quotation marks. In order to use this methodology to create an e-mail link simply use this:

```
<A HREF="mailto:somebody@somemail.com">
```

You simply have to change the "http://" portion to "mailto:". Notice that all three of the preceding methods have one thing in common. They do not close the command in the typical manner that other HTML commands are closed. Now let's examine the source code for a simple but complete HTML document:

**Example 1-2**

```
<HTML>
<HEAD>
   <TITLE>Test HTML Page</TITLE>
</HEAD>
<BODY BGCOLOR="blue">
<P>
```

```
>My First Web Page </FONT></B></CENTER>
<B><I>LOVE</I></B> HTML!
ript.jpg" ></CENTER>

at</CENTER>

mail@someemail.com">Email ME</A>

lisher's Web Site </CENTER>
ww.wordware.com">WordWare Publishing</A></CENTER>
```

should note at the beginning a new command:

d color of your page using this command and any
t a background image for your HTML document

```
if">
```

ilable in the code files in a folder named Chap-
roperly and used the image supplied, your web
something like Figure 1-2.

Figure 1-2

Now I will be the first to admit that this sample web page is very trivial. But it does contain the basics of HTML. With the material we have covered so far you can display images, texts, links, e-mail links, background colors, and background images. Not too bad for just a few short pages.

## Colors and Backgrounds

Let's examine a few other simple items we can add to our HTML documents. The first is altering text color. You can set the default text color for the entire document and you can alter the color of specific text. You alter the default text color for the entire document using a technique very similar to the one used to alter the background color:

```
<BODY TEXT="blue">
```

This text simply tells the browser that unless otherwise specified, all text in this document should be blue. In addition to changing the default color of all text in a document you may wish to simply change the color of a specific section of text. This is fairly easy to do as well. Instead of using the BODY TEXT command we use the FONT command:

```
<FONT COLOR="red">This is red text</FONT>
```

This, like the other color commands, can be used with any standard color. There are a wide variety of tags you can use to alter the appearance and behavior of text and images. Just a few others for you to consider would be the <BLINK> </BLINK> tag which, as the name implies, causes the text to blink (this is only supported by Netscape and will not work in Internet Explorer). Another example is <STRIKE> </STRIKE>, which causes the text to appear with a line through it, a strike through. The tags we have covered so far are enough to allow you to accomplish what you need in HTML.

# Tables

The next HTML command we are going to examine is the table. They are a very good way to organize data on your web page. You can use tables with or without a border. I will explain the various reasons to use one method or the other.

First I will show you how to create a table with a border:

**Example 1-3A**

```
<TABLE BORDER=1>
    <TR>
        <TD>
            <P>This
            <P>Is a
    <TR>
        <TD>
            <P>Table
        <TD>
            <P>With a border
</TABLE>
```

By now you should be able to recognize that the <TABLE> and </TABLE> tags actually contain the table. Each <TR> tag designates another row in the table. The <TD> tag creates a cell within that row (TD refers to table data). Using those three tags you can create a table with any number of rows or columns you wish. Notice that the first line of this code has the BORDER property set to 1. This means the border has a width and is therefore visible.

In some instances you may not want the border to show. Tables can be used simply to hold images and text in relative positions. In cases such as this you may not wish to have a visible border. Below is an example of a table whose borders will not show.

**Example 1-3B**

```
<P><TABLE BORDER=0 CELLSPACING=0 CELLPADDING=0>
    <TR>
        <TD>
            <P>This
        <TD>
            <P>is a
    <TR>
        <TD>
```

```
                <P>Table
        <TD>
                <P>With no borders or padding
    </TABLE>
```

Notice that the BORDER, CELLPADDING, and CELLSPACING properties are all set to 0. This causes the table itself to not be displayed. However, the contents of the table will display. You should also notice that in both examples I have placed text in each cell.

Figure 1-3 shows two tables, one with a border and one without.

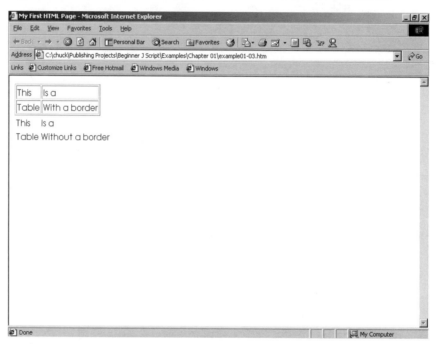

Figure 1-3

Since the entire purpose of this book is to teach you JavaScript, the obvious question on your mind should be "How do I insert scripts into HTML?" Well, fortunately, that is not particularly difficult. The browser deals with script code (including JavaScript) like it handles HTML code, scanning the source from left to right and from top to bottom. JavaScript has "tags" of its own by which it instructs the browser and determines the layout. However, JavaScript is not read exactly like HTML. In HTML, the browser acts immediately according to the elements it recognizes. Not all JavaScript code refers to actions that take place while the page is loading. Some parts are just kept in memory until they are called. For instance, if you write a function and do not call it, the browser does not do anything with it. This part of the script stays in memory and can be invoked later. But the real question you are likely wondering about before you proceed with the rest of this book and learning JavaScript is, how do you put scripts into your HTML documents. Any script can be placed in a document very easily by encasing the script inside of two commands:

```
<SCRIPT LANGUAGE = "whateverscriptlanguageyouareusing">
```

and

```
</SCRIPT>
```

There is a variety of scripting languages available for the web including VBScript (based on the Visual Basic programming language), CGI, and of course, JavaScript. Below are two examples of JavaScripts inserted into HTML code.

```
<SCRIPT LANGUAGE="JavaScript">
document.write("<IMG SRC='img4-2.gif' ALT='pencil icon' HEIGHT=71 WIDTH=53>")
</SCRIPT>

<SCRIPT LANGUAGE="JavaScript">
function makeDialogBox()
{
    alert("Wonderful!")
}
</SCRIPT>
```

## Lists

It is common to present data in lists. With HTML you have access to a variety of types of lists. The first we will discuss is the unordered list shown below.

```
<UL>
    <LI> First Item
    <LI> Second Item
</UL>
```

The <UL> and </UL> tags define the code that lies between them as being part of an unordered list. The <LI> tags identify list items. An unordered list item will simply appear as a bulleted item, as shown in the following figure.

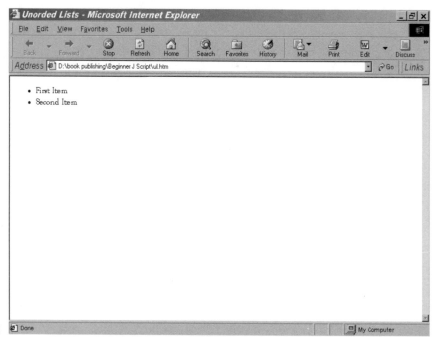

Figure 1-4

An ordered list is not much different. The <LI> list item stays the same. But the <UL> is going to change somewhat.

```
<OL type = I>
    <LI> First Item
    <LI> Second Item
</OL>
```

The "type =" portion of the tag tells the browser what type of list this is. We used a capital I in our example, which will give you capital roman numerals for your list items.

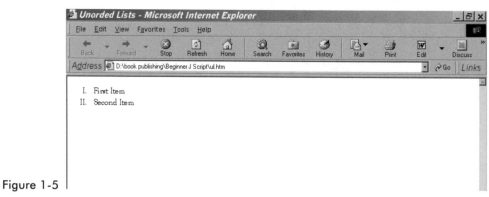

Figure 1-5

The following table shows all the types of ordered lists and how they appear in your browser.

| | |
|---|---|
| Type = I | I. First Item<br>II. Second Item |
| Type = i | i. First Item<br>ii. Second Item |
| Type = 1 | 1. First Item<br>2. Second Item |
| Type = a | a. First Item<br>b. Second Item |
| Type = A | A. First Item<br>B. Second Item |

See Example 1-4 in the code for a demonstration of lists.

## Marquee

A very fascinating item you can add to your web page is the marquee. A scrolling marquee takes a message or an image and scrolls it across the screen. The basic format is this:

```
<MARQUEE LOOP = INFINITE> Hey this is really cool </MARQUEE>
```

In addition to text, you can also place an image in the marquee to scroll across the screen:

```
<MARQUEE LOOP = INFINITE> <IMG SRC = "mypic.gif"></MARQUEE>
```

You can also change the direction the marquee moves in. The <DIRECTION> tag will tell the marquee which direction to scroll to, not from.

```
<MARQUEE LOOP = INFINITE DIRECTION = RIGHT>Hey this is a cool marquee </MARQUEE>
```

You can choose from the following directions: Left, Right, Up, and Down. Marquees provide an interesting and relatively easy way to display eye-catching information on your web page.

## Summary

Let me stress that what I have just covered with you are simply the essentials of writing HTML code. You can find a number of books that will go into HTML in more depth than this.

There are also a variety of software packages that will do the HTML code for you. You simply create a document just as you would in any word processor and the software will create the underlying HTML code. Two very inexpensive options that I recommend for basic HTML coding are Claris Works Home Page (about $25) and Netscape Composer, which comes with Netscape Communicator and is absolutely free of charge.

# Chapter 2

# JavaScript Primer

This book will teach you JavaScript by walking you step by step through the production of a complete web site. However, to get a jump start it is essential that you first have a basic grasp of JavaScript. The goal of this chapter is to introduce you to the basic concepts of JavaScript. Each of the successive chapters discusses a particular facet of JavaScript with several examples. Just before the summary of each of the following chapters is a section where we use the material covered in that chapter for the web site we are building.

This chapter will take you into the technical details of JavaScript. It is possible to read the later chapters and use them without reading this chapter. However, at some point you will want to review this chapter. Its contents explain the intricacies of how JavaScript works. Even if you skip this chapter, I recommend you come back to it when you have read the first 10 chapters of the book.

## Essential Tools

HTML files are plain text files. Therefore, in order to add JavaScript to an existing HTML document, you need a text editor. Notepad is an excellent choice for a simple text editor, if for no other reason than it's free with Windows. Most operating systems including Windows, Macintosh, and Linux come with a free text editor.

You can use various editors for your JavaScript as well as your HTML. However, many experienced web developers simply use a standard text editor that usually comes free with their operating system. If you are using Windows, you already have Notepad and WordPad on your PC; those are both fine for doing HTML and JavaScript. The advantage of using standard text editors is that they are free. The disadvantage is that they do not offer any debugging tools to help you with the JavaScript. I personally prefer simply using Notepad for my HTML and JavaScript development.

### Choosing a Browser

Besides the basic programming tool, you need to be able to run your scripts and view their output. It doesn't really matter which browser you choose. The latest versions of Netscape and Microsoft Internet Explorer both fully support JavaScript. Compatibility should only be a serious problem with older versions of browsers. Since both browsers are available as a free download, it is probably advisable that you download a copy of both so that you can test your scripts in both.

## Basic JavaScript Structure

In order to run client-side JavaScript, you must embed the code in the HTML document. However, you cannot place JavaScript statements in the source code in just any location. There are basically two methods to embed JavaScript scripts in HTML:

- As statements and functions using the <SCRIPT> </SCRIPT> tags.
- As short statements resembling URLs.

### The <SCRIPT> Tag

This tag defines in HTML that a script follows. You can declare a script that is directly written in the HTML code, or in a separate file.

#### Internal Scripts

The <SCRIPT> tag is used to enclose JavaScript code in HTML documents. This is the most common way to include simple JavaScripts and it is the method we will use for most of this book. Here is the general syntax:

```
<SCRIPT LANGUAGE="JavaScript">
[JavaScript Statements...]
</SCRIPT>
```

The <SCRIPT LANGUAGE="JavaScript"> tag acts like all other HTML tags. Notice that it must be followed by its closing counterpart, </SCRIPT>. Every statement you put between the two tags will be interpreted as JavaScript code. This is probably the most common method for inserting JavaScript into HTML documents.

The LANGUAGE attribute is used to specify the scripting language. At present, the <SCRIPT> tag supports various languages including JavaScript and VBScript. JavaScript is the default scripting language, so the LANGUAGE definition is not required. However, I recommend that you still use it for the sake of clarity. When the browser comes across the precise name of the language, it loads the built-in JavaScript interpreter and then interprets the script.

JavaScript is case sensitive, but HTML is not. It does not matter whether you write <SCRIPT> or <script>, but try to be consistent. Be sure to write the name of the language properly. Personally I use all capitals in my HTML; even though it does not matter to the browser, it does to the person reading my HTML code. You will find that many web developers follow this convention. Remember that HTML and JavaScript are no different from any programming language in that you should always strive to make sure your code is readable.

**2**

Chapter

### External Scripts

There is a SRC attribute for the <SCRIPT> tag, which enables the use of external scripts. This means you can place your script in a separate file and include it using the SRC attribute. External scripts are useful when you have lengthy or complex scripts and you feel that including them directly in your HTML code would make for difficult reading. I will be using external scripts later in this book.

## Placing JavaScript Code

When you want to place the script somewhere in the HTML document, you need to choose an appropriate place to put it. Technically, you may place it anywhere between the <HTML> and </HTML> tags that enclose the whole document. Actually, the two possibilities are the <HEAD>...</HEAD> portion and the <BODY>...</BODY> portion. Because the <HEAD>... </HEAD> portion is evaluated first, many developers choose to place their JavaScript here. A single HTML document may contain any number of scripts. You can place some of the scripts in the <HEAD>...</HEAD> portion, and others in the <BODY>...</BODY> portion of the page. The choice of where to place them should follow some logic based on when you wish the script to execute. Script placed in the <HEAD> section will be executed as soon as the web page is loaded. The following code demonstrates this:

```
<HTML>
<HEAD>
<TITLE>Using Multiple scripts</TITLE>
<SCRIPT LANGUAGE="JavaScript">
[JavaScript statements...]
</SCRIPT>
<SCRIPT LANGUAGE="JavaScript">
[JavaScript statements...]
</SCRIPT>
</HEAD>
<BODY>
<H1>This is another script</H1>
<SCRIPT LANGUAGE="JavaScript">
[JavaScript statements...]
</SCRIPT>
</BODY>
</HTML>
```

## JavaScript Conventions

There are several conventions used to make JavaScript code more understandable. Some of these are discussed in this section.

### Using the Semicolon

The JavaScript interpreter does not pay any attention to carriage return characters in the source. It is possible to put numerous statements on the same line, but you must separate them with a semicolon (;). You can also add a semicolon at the end of a statement that occupies its own line, but it is not necessary. Take a look at the following statements:

```
document.write("Hello"); alert("Good bye")
```

```
document.write("Hello")
alert("Good bye")
```

```
document.write("Hello");
alert("Good bye");
```

All three sets are legal, and their results are identical. Let me stress that the semicolons are not needed; I just mention them because programmers whose background is C, C++, or Java will be used to ending their statements with a semicolon. Although the semicolon is allowed, I personally never use it, since its use is superfluous in JavaScript.

### Case Sensitivity

It was mentioned previously in this chapter that JavaScript is a case-sensitive language. This fact applies to all aspects of the language, including variable names (*identifiers*), functions, and methods (discussed later). The statement document.write(), for example, is legal, but document.Write() is not.

### Comments

Comments are an important concept in all languages, including in JavaScript. They help make programs simple and easy to understand. Comments are messages that can be put into programs at various points without affecting the results. There are two different types of comments in JavaScript:

- Single-line comments are comments that do not exceed the length of one line. These comments begin with a double slash (//).

- Multiple-line comments are comments that exceed the length of one line. Therefore, they require a sign that specifies the beginning of the comment, and another sign that specifies the end of the comment. The opening part is /* and the closing part is */.

```
// single-line comment
/* line 1 of the multi line comment
   line 2 of the multi line comment
   line 3 of the multi line comment */
```

Both types of comments are identical to the comments in Java, C, and C++.

Comments are an essential part of any programming language. If you work in a team environment, comments will allow others to clearly understand the intentions of your code. I would also add that if you review your own code several months after writing it, you are unlikely to remember exactly what you where planning. Although some programmers will state that very well-written code needs few or no comments, I strongly disagree with this. I personally advocate a very liberal use of comments in your code. Even if you "over-comment," absolutely no harm is done.

### Using Quotes

In JavaScript, you often use quotes to accomplish various goals, such as delimiting strings. A common problem arises when using a pair of quotes inside another pair of quotes. Since the interpreter must recognize each set of quotes in order to pair them correctly, the creators of JavaScript made it possible to use two different types of quotes: double quotes (") and single quotes ('). If you need only one set of quotes, you can choose either of them as long as

**2**

Chapter

you terminate the text with the same type of quote you used to open it. If you use quotes improperly, you will get a JavaScript error: "unterminated string literal." You must make certain that you alternate quotes properly:

```
document.write("<IMG SRC='cool.gif'>")
```

## Your First Script

Now that you have read about the basic concepts behind JavaScript, I think it is time to actually write a little JavaScript. You are probably quite bored with all this background information and eager to see some action.

First of all, launch your text editor. Type Example 2-1 in the text editor and save it under the name Hello.htm. Make sure the name ends with either the .htm or .html extension, or your browser will not recognize this as an HTML document. It is imperative, however, that as you type in this example you make every attempt to fully understand what it is you are typing. Next, launch the browser. Since the file is local, you do not need to be connected to the Internet to view the results. Now, load the file from the browser's menu. That's all there is to it. You can start enjoying JavaScript.

The following script is interpreted and executed immediately when you load the page containing it.

**Example 2-1**

```
<HTML>
<HEAD>
<TITLE>Hello World.</TITLE>
</HEAD>
<BODY>
<SCRIPT LANGUAGE="JavaScript">
<!--hide code from old browsers
document.write("<H1>Hello World.</H1>")
// end code hiding
</SCRIPT>
</BODY>
</HTML>
```

If you entered the code properly you should see something in your browser similar to Figure 2-1.

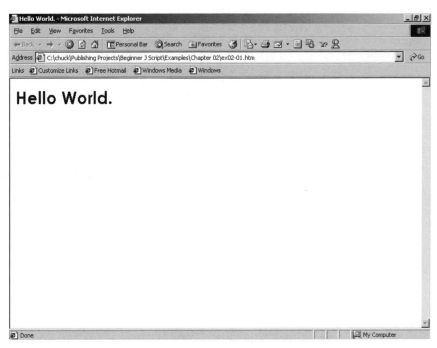

Figure 2-1

This example is OK, but I personally prefer using JavaScript alert boxes. So let us rewrite Example 2-1 using an alert box:

**Example 2-2**

```
<HTML>
<HEAD>
<TITLE>Hello Again!</TITLE>
</HEAD>
<BODY>
<SCRIPT LANGUAGE="JavaScript">
<!--hide code from old browsers
  alert("Hello World")
// end code hiding
</SCRIPT>
</BODY>
</HTML>
```

These two, very basic JavaScripts should give you a feel for the language, and hopefully whet your appetite to learn more. However, before we can delve into the exciting world of building dynamic web sites with JavaScript, we need to cover the more mundane fundamentals of the language.

# Fundamental JavaScript Concepts

JavaScript is composed of the same basic elements as all programming languages. It has variables, which hold data, it has expressions or statements, and it has functions. Each of these building blocks are used to construct your JavaScript.

## Data Types and Variables in JavaScript

Variables are essentially named segments of memory set aside to hold data of a certain type. These types are referred to as data types. When you create a variable you are simply allocating a space in memory for the data type of the variable you declare. It is important to use the proper data type to store your information. For example, a number is a type of information that JavaScript recognizes. Compared to most programming languages, JavaScript has a small number of data types. There are only four different data types in JavaScript: numbers, strings, Boolean, and null values. As opposed to other languages, a variable data type is not declared explicitly but rather implicitly according to its initial value assignment. Also unique to JavaScript is the lack of an explicit distinction between integer and real-valued numbers.

JavaScript is a *loosely typed* language. The only keyword for declaring a JavaScript variable is var. The actual data type used depends on the initial value you assign to the variable. Consider the following examples:

```
var LastName = "Smith"
var AccountNumber = 1111
```

In the first example, the data type of LastName is string, simply because that is the initial value assigned to that variable. In the second example, the data type of AccountNumber is number.

This method of variable declaration is in stark contrast with *strongly typed* languages such as C or Java. In strongly typed languages the variable must be created of a specific type.

```
int myint:
boolean myboolean;
```

There are a few rules to observe when creating variables:

■ The first character cannot be a digit.

■ All other characters can be letters, underscores, or digits (0-9).

■ An identifier cannot be one of the language's reserved words. Reserved words are basically the words that make up the JavaScript language.

■ JavaScript is case sensitive (uppercase letters are distinct from lowercase letters). For example, counter, Counter, and COUNTER are the names of three different variables. Avoid using such similar identifiers in the same script.

The following variable names are legal:

```
loopcounter
_employeename
_123456789_
account_number
Number16
```

but the following ones are illegal:

```
with                  // reserved word
^mystring             // first character is illegal
411information        // cannot start with a digit
04-825-6408           // first character is illegal
                      // "-" is an illegal character
***important***       // * is not a legal character
```

The action of assigning an initial value to a variable is called *initialization*. You give the variable a value using the *assignment operator*—the equal sign:

```
var variableName = initialValue
```

You only need to use the var keyword when you create the variable. When you want to refer to the variable, you only use its name. Assign a value to a variable (after it has been declared) in the following fashion:

```
variableName = anyValue
```

You use var only once per variable. A global variable can be created simply by assigning it a value without the var keyword. Local variables inside functions, on the other hand, must be declared with the var keyword. As in many other programming languages, JavaScript allows you to declare numerous variables in the same statement, using a comma to separate them:

```
var variableName1 = initialValue1, variableName2 = initialValue2, …
```

2

Chapter

## JavaScript Operators

Every programming language has operators. An operator is simply a symbol that tells the compiler (or interpreter) to perform a certain action. The basic arithmetic operators are common to most programming languages. These are addition (+), subtraction (–), multiplication (*), and division (/). These should be very familiar to most people. The order of precedence of operators follows the standard mathematical rules of multiplication, division, addition, and subtraction. However, when your code has multiple operations in a single line it is usually a good idea to use parentheses to clarify what you want to occur; 3 * 4/2 + 1 can be ambiguous, whereas 3 * ( (4/2) + 1) is very clear.

C, C++, and Java programmers will already be familiar with the increment and decrement operators, while other programmers may not be. The increment operator is done by placing two plus signs after a variable, such as this:

```
Var somenumber
Somenumber++
```

This line of code increments the value of somenumber by one. Had we written:

```
somenumber --
```

it would have decreased the value by one.

It is very important that you realize that where you place the increment and decrement operators is critical. If you place the increment operator after a variable such as:

```
Var somenumber = 10
Var someothernumber
Someothernumber = somenumber++
```

The assignment operation will take place before the evaluation operation. In other words, first someothernumber will be set equal to the value of somenumber then the value of somenumber will be incremented. In our example that means that someothernumber will equal 10 and somenumber will equal 11. If you wish to rewrite the statement so that the increment takes place first, just reposition the increment sign:

```
Someothernumber = ++somenumber
```

In this case, somenumber is incremented to 11 and then that value is assigned to someothernumber.

You've already learned how to assign a value to a variable or to initialize it using the equal assignment operator. As the following piece of code demonstrates, you can also perform calculations when you assign a value:

```
/* 1 */ var answer
/* 2 */ answer = 4 * 2 + 9
/* 3 */ document.write(answer)
```

Line 1 includes the declaration of the variable answer. The second line shows how the variable answer is assigned the result of a simple mathematical expression. At this point, the variable holds a value of 17. Referring to the variable answer is the same as referring to the number 17. For this reason, the statement on line 3 prints the number 17.

**CAUTION:** A common mistake is to use the equal sign for equality check. In Visual Basic, for example, = is an equality test operator, because the basic assignment operator of the language is :=. However, in JavaScript, like in C++ and Java, = (the equal sign) is an assignment operator, while == (two equal signs) is an equality test operator.

## JavaScript Statements

Now that we have thoroughly examined data types, let's look at statements. A *statement* is simply a line of code that performs some specific task or action. For example, all of the following are statements:

```
myAge = 32
for(x=1;x<10,x++)
myname= "Chuck"
```

### Multiple Statements

The JavaScript interpreter accepts multiple statements on the same line. If you choose to use this method, you must separate the statements with semicolons (;). Note that this is the only place in JavaScript where you are required to use the semicolon, and, in my opinion, the only place you should use it. The last statement of the line does not have to be followed by a semicolon. Such a line looks like this:

```
statement1; statement2; statement3; ...
```

The browser interprets these statements as if they were on separate lines:

```
statement1
statement2
statement3
```

Although this is possible with JavaScript I certainly do not recommend it. Placing multiple statements on a single line makes for very unreadable code.

### Nested Statements

A command block is a unit of statements enclosed by curly braces. It is very important to understand that a block should be used as a single statement. The statements inside the block are called *nested statements*:

```
{
      nested statement1
      nested statement2
      nested statement3
}
```

A loop that includes many statements is actually one statement with many nested statements. This rule applies to functions, if-else statements, and other language elements.

## JavaScript Expressions

Now that you know how to create a variable, you need to know how to use it. As mentioned earlier, variables hold values of different types. What does "holding a value" mean? This term refers to expression *evaluation*. A variable always evaluates to its value. When you perform an operation on a variable, you are actually performing the operation on the current value associated with the variable. Let's assume you created a variable named firstNumber using the following statement:

```
var firstNumber = 120 // declaration and initialization
```

At this point, if you refer to the variable firstNumber, its value, 120, is returned. That is, firstNumber is evaluated to 120. The following statement outlines an evaluation of firstNumber:

```
secondNumber = firstNumber * 6
```

The secondNumber variable now holds the value 720, because firstNumber evaluates to 120. Bear in mind that no link between the memory locations of the variables is established. Therefore, secondNumber now holds a value of 720, which does not change even if the value of firstNumber changes. A variable can evaluate to a value of any type.

## JavaScript Function Declarations

A *function* is simply a group of related statements that perform some common goal and are grouped together under some common function name. Just like variables, you must define a function before you can call it.

Functions are defined using the keyword function, followed by the name of the function. The same rules that apply to naming variables apply to naming functions. Since a function usually does something besides storing a value, it is common to include a verb in its name. The most important thing to remember about naming functions is that the name should provide some indication of what the function does. The function's parameters are written in brackets after the name. Parameters are simply values that are passed into a function for the function to process. The syntax of a function definition is:

```
function functionName([parameters])
{
    [statements]
}
```

*Parameters* are local variables that are assigned values when the function is called. At this point, you should always give a name to every parameter.

In a formal syntax specification, the square brackets "[" and "]" usually denote optional elements. Since a function does not have to have parameters or statements, they are both enclosed in such brackets. The curly braces enclosing the function body can be placed anywhere, following the parameter section. The following functions are valid:

```
function functionName([parameters]) {[statement1]; [statement2]; …}
function functionName([parameters])
{
    [statement1]
    [statement2]
}
```

The following example demonstrates a function declaration:

### Example 2-3

```
<HTML>
<HEAD>
<SCRIPT LANGUAGE="JavaScript">
<!-- hide script contents from old browsers
function square(number)
```

```
        {
            document.write("The call passed ",number, // the function's parameter
                " to the function.<BR>",
                number,                                 // the function's parameter
                " square is ",
                number * number,
                ".<BR>")
        }
// *** add function call
// end hiding contents from old browsers  -->
</SCRIPT>
</HEAD>
<BODY>
</BODY>
</HTML>
```

Example 2-3 does not print anything to the browser's window, nor does it generate any other form of output. The reason is that the function is only defined in the script but never called. When the browser locates a function, it loads its statements into the memory, ready to be executed later.

### Calling Functions

In order to execute the set of statements located in the function block, you must call the function. The syntax of a function call is:

```
functionName([arguments])
```

By adding the statement square(5) to Example 2-2, at the specified place, we call the function. The statements in the function are executed, and the following message is output:

```
The call passed 5 to the function.
5 square is 25.
```

You can also call a function from within another function, as the following example demonstrates:

### Example 2-4

```
<HTML>
<HEAD>
<TITLE>Calling a function from within another function</TITLE>
<SCRIPT LANGUAGE="JavaScript">
<!-- hide script contents from old browsers
function makeBar()
{
    var output = "<HR ALIGN='left' WIDTH=400>"
```

```
        document.write(output)
    }
    function makeHeader(text, color, size)
    {
        var output = "<FONT COLOR='" + color + "' SIZE=" +
            size + ">" + text + "</FONT>"
        document.write(output)
         makeBar()
    }
    makeHeader("JavaScript Examples", "red", "+4")
    // end hiding contents from old browsers  -->
    </SCRIPT>
    </HEAD>
    <BODY>
    </BODY>
    </HTML>
```

Example 2-4 summarizes many of the terms discussed in this chapter. It includes two function definitions. In both functions, the output is assigned to a variable (output) and then printed to the client window using the document.write() method. Assigning strings to variables before printing them is extremely useful when the string is long (you want to print a lot of data). You can see the result of Example 2-3 in the following image.

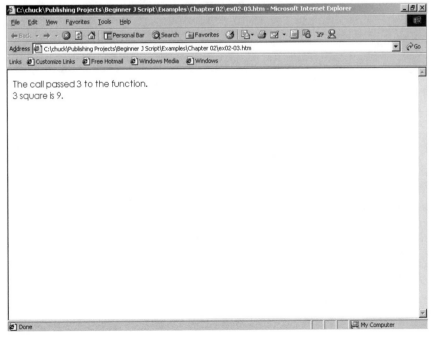

Figure 2-2

# Dialog Boxes

JavaScript provides the ability to create small windows called *dialog boxes*. You can create small alert boxes, confirm boxes, and prompt boxes. These boxes let you generate output and receive input from the user.

## Alert Boxes

An alert box is the most simple dialog box. It enables you to display a short message to the user in a separate window. Take a look at the following script and its corresponding output:

```
alert("Click OK to continue...")
```

The generic form of this function is alert(*message*). The function alert() is actually a method of the window object. It is not necessary to specify that because window is the default object. The same applies to all dialog boxes.

**NOTE:** Netscape Communications Corp. implemented the "JavaScript Alert:." header for security reasons. It is used to distinguish JavaScript dialog boxes from those created by the operating system, so that the user knows what the source of the message is. JavaScript programmers cannot trick the user into doing something he might not want to do. It also disables the ability to scare the user into giving out personal information.

You can also display messages using variables. For example:

```
var message = "Click OK to continue"
alert(message)
```

The alert box is often used to pause the execution of a script until the user approves its continuation.

## Confirm Boxes

Confirm boxes are different from alert boxes in that they evaluate to a value based on a decision made by the user. Rather than a simple OK button, the confirm box includes both OK and Cancel buttons.

Like the alert box, confirm is also a method of the window object. This method returns a Boolean value, because there are two options. You can use confirmation boxes to ask the user a yes-or-no question, or to confirm an action. Here is an example and its output:

```
var reply = confirm("OK to continue?")
```

reply is assigned a true value if the user chooses OK, and false if the user selects Cancel. The generic form of this function is confirm(*message*).

## Prompt Boxes

The prompt() method displays a prompt dialog box with a message and an input field. You can use these boxes to receive input from the user. It is similar to the confirm box, except that it returns the value of the input field, rather than true or false. Here is an example:

```
var name = prompt("Enter your name:", "anonymous")
```

The method returns a value of null if the user chooses Cancel. The prompt box looks like the image shown in Figure 2-3.

Figure 2-3

The value of the field is always a string. If the user enters 16 in the form, the string "16" is returned rather than the number 16. When you want to prompt the user for a number, you must convert the input into a numeric value. JavaScript features a built-in function that does this—parseInt(). You can use the following statement to ask the user for a number:

```
var number = parseInt(prompt("Enter a number:", 0))
```

or

```
var number = prompt("Enter a number:", 0)
number = parseInt(number)
```

The generic form of this function is prompt(message[, inputDefault]).

You can see that this function works by using the typeof operator for testing:

```
var number = prompt("Enter a number:", 0)
alert(number, " is a ", typeof number) // "... is a string"
number = parseInt(number)
alert(number, " is a ", typeof number) // "... is a number"
```

The input must be of a numeric type, of course (e.g., 99).

# if Statement

```
if (condition)
    statement
```

The if statement lets you put decision making in your scripts. A script without any decisions does the same procedure each time it is executed. Such linear structures limit your scripts to simple algorithms. JavaScript enables decision making using an if statement. if statements associate a single statement with a true condition. That statement is only executed if the conditional expression is true; otherwise it is not executed at all. The condition must evaluate to a Boolean value: true or false. Numeric values are also acceptable as an alternative to a Boolean condition. 0 is equivalent to false, and all other values are equivalent to true.

The if statement associates a single statement with a true condition. A statement can be anything from a simple document.write() to a block of statements using curly braces ({}). Some if statements require multiple statements, so they use a block in the following form:

```
if (condition)
{
    statement1
    statement2
    statement3
}
<HTML>
<HEAD>
<TITLE>A simple if statement</TITLE>
<SCRIPT LANGUAGE="JavaScript">
<!--
var age = parseInt(prompt("Please enter your age:", 15))
if (age > 30)
    alert("Wow, you are old enough to remember Disco!")
// -->
</SCRIPT>
</HEAD>
<BODY>
    JavaScript Example
</BODY>
</HTML>
```

This is a simple HTML document that includes a JavaScript script. And admittedly it is nothing to get overly excited about. However, it does illustrate exactly how to place JavaScript into an HTML document. Notice that its structure is the same as that of any other HTML document. The only new concept is the <SCRIPT> tag. I put the script in the <BODY>...</BODY> portion of the page, though you may put it anywhere between the <HTML> and </HTML> tags. For now, think of document.write() as a way to print expressions to the page. write() is actually a method of the document object. Objects, methods, and properties are introduced in Chapter 6, "The Document Object Model." The write() method supports any HTML syntax. Be aware, also, that all strings must be included in quotes.

## Summary

This chapter showed you the basics of JavaScript. This, combined with the HTML primer, should give you the foundational skills necessary to follow the rest of this book. Make sure you are totally comfortable with the material in these first two chapters before proceeding.

**2**

Chapter

# Alerts, Prompts, and User Feedback

Before you continue with this book, make sure that you are thoroughly familiar with the material in Chapters 1 and 2. That material provides the fundamental building blocks that I will use throughout the rest of the book to guide you through building a complete web site. Without a basic grasp of HTML and the fundamentals of JavaScript, it will be difficult for you to work through the rest of this book.

For educational purposes I am going to walk you through the process of building a complete web site for a fictitious business. Since I happen to enjoy antique book collecting, we are going to build a web site for an antique bookstore. However, the techniques are common to all businesses. Each chapter will first discuss a particular technique or techniques and then give you some examples using those techniques. Then the chapter will use one or more of them demonstrated in our ficticious business web site we are building.

## Alert Boxes

One of the simplest things to do with JavaScript is the alert box. An alert box is simply a small message box that pops up and gives the user some information. Let's start by adding a simple greeting to visitors. This greeting will be jazzed up as we go along, with more interesting features.

Consider the following example:

**Example 3-1**

```
<HTML>
<HEAD>
    <TITLE>Alert Box</TITLE>
```

33

```
<SCRIPT LANGUAGE="JavaScript">
    function alertMe(message)
    {
      alert(message)
    }
alertMe("Welcome to my web page!")
</SCRIPT>
</HEAD>
<BODY>
</BODY>
</HTML>
```

This may seem like a rather trivial item to add to a web page, but you should note two things. The first is that some simple pop-up boxes and dynamic content can easily differentiate your web site from others. The second thing you should keep in mind is that this script shows you how to use alert boxes. An alert box is a built-in JavaScript function that allows you to display messages to the user. All you have to pass it is either a variable or a literal string value you want to display. You will see, throughout this book, that this is a very useful technique and will be used frequently.

If you entered the code correctly for Example 3-1 you should see this image:

Figure 3-1

# Prompt Boxes

Now we are going to expand this script to use a prompt box, and to have different action depending on the user's response. A prompt box is very similar to an alert box, only it allows the user to enter in data. The following script gives you a basic idea of how a prompt box works.

**Example 3-2**

```
<HTML>
<HEAD>
    <TITLE>Prompt Box</TITLE>
<SCRIPT LANGUAGE="JavaScript">
<!--
var name = prompt("Please Enter your name:", "John Doe")
alert("Hello " + name)
// -->
</SCRIPT>
</HEAD>
<BODY>
</BODY>
</HTML>
```

This script begins by using a prompt box to inquire as to the user's name. The value of the user's input is placed into a variable called name using the assignment operator = (remember that a single = assigns a value to a variable whereas a == evaluates whether or not a variable is equal to a particular value).

```
var name = prompt("Please Enter your name:", "John Doe")
```

Please note that we do provide the user with a default value, in case he or she does not enter any value. Then we simply display a greeting to the web site visitor using the name he or she just provided. The following figures show these prompt boxes.

**3**

Chapter

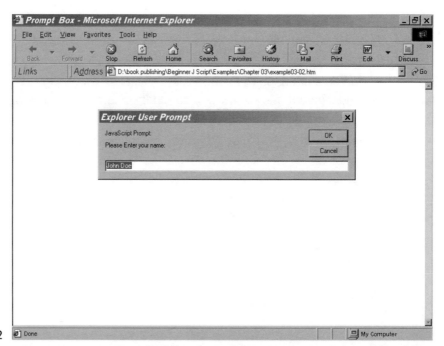

Figure 3-2

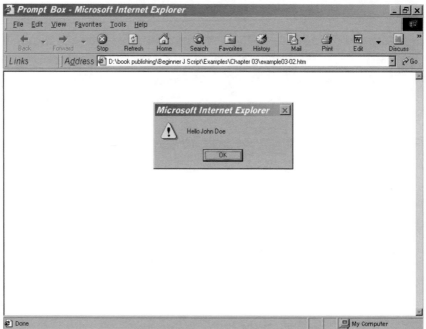

Figure 3-3

The next example demonstrates the use of a prompt box in conjunction with an alert box and an if statement. This script asks the user what browser he or she is using and responds accordingly.

The next thing we ask the user to do is to indicate whether or not he or she is using a recent version of their browser. You should notice, by this point, that all input boxes have OK and Cancel buttons. If the user clicks Cancel, the variable that is assigned the value of the prompt will contain a null value. Also notice that the only structural difference between the two prompt boxes is the use of the word "prompt" prior to the parenthesis.

```
var name = prompt("Please Enter your name:", "John Doe")
var message = "Click OK if you are using Netscape 3.0 or above, or Internet
Explorer 4.0 or above"
```

If you place the word prompt before the opening parenthesis, JavaScript will create a text field in the prompt box it displays, so that the user can enter data. Without the prompt command, your prompt box will only allow the user to choose between OK and Cancel.

The second question is to make sure the user has a recent version of their browser. Older browsers do not support all of the JavaScript commands we might use in the creation of our web site. After the user tells us whether or not he or she has a recent version, we use an if statement to choose our next course of action.

```
if (!confirm(message))
{
alert("Please download the latest version of Netscape or Internet Explorer.")
}
else
{
        alert ("Hello " + name )
}
```

The following simple script illustrates for you the use of alert boxes and two different types of prompt boxes, combined with an if-else code segment to create a useful addition to our web site.

**Example 3-3**

```
<HTML>
<HEAD>
   <TITLE>Prompt box 2</TITLE>
<SCRIPT LANGUAGE="JavaScript">
<!--
```

**3**

Chapter

```
var name = prompt("Please Enter your name:", "John Doe")
var message = "Click OK if you are using Netscape 5.0 or above, or Internet
Explorer 5.0 or above"
if (!confirm(message))
{
   alert("Please download the latest version of Netscape or Internet Explorer.")
}
else
{
        alert ("Hello " + name )
}
// -->
</SCRIPT>
</HEAD>
<BODY>

</BODY>
</HTML>
```

# Writing Back to the Web Page

Alert boxes and prompt boxes are fairly easy methods for providing some level of user interaction. You can also use JavaScript to write information directly back onto the web page. Essentially, an alert box is perfect if you wish to display something and then have it disappear as soon as the user acknowledges it. However, if you want information to stay on the screen the entire time the user is on your site, then you need to write that to the actual HTML document.

If we replace the previous script with the following one we will be able to retain the current user's name on the page for as long as they are visiting the site.

**Example 3-4**

```
<HTML>
<HEAD>
   <TITLE>Writing to the web page</TITLE>
<SCRIPT LANGUAGE="JavaScript">
<!--
var name = prompt("Please Enter your name:", "John Doe")
var message = "Click OK if you are using Netscape 3.0 or above, or Internet
Explorer 4.0 or above"
if (!confirm(message))
{
```

```
        alert("Please download the latest version of Netscape or Internet Explorer.")
}
else
{
        document.write(name)
}
// -->
</SCRIPT>
</HEAD>
<BODY BGCOLOR= White>
</BODY>
</HTML>
```

Note that the only real difference is this segment:

```
else
{
        document.write(name)
}
```

Instead of putting up an alert box, we write the user's name onto the actual web page. Notice the use of the document object. This object represents the web page that is currently loaded into the browser. You can do a lot of interesting things with this object, as you will see. Now writing a line to the HTML page is moderately interesting. But what is more interesting is the fact that you can use the document.write() method to actually write new HTML into the document. Take a look at this example:

**Example 3-5**

```
<HTML>
<HEAD>
   <TITLE>Writing to the web page</TITLE>
<SCRIPT LANGUAGE="JavaScript">
var name = prompt("Please Enter M if you are male and F if you are female", "M")
if(name=='M')
{
        document.write('<FONT COLOR = Blue>')
        document.write('<H1>Yo Dude!</H1>')
        document.write('</FONT>')

}
else
{
        document.write('<FONT COLOR =Pink>')
        document.write('<H1>You go girl!</H1>')
        document.write('</FONT>')
```

Chapter **3**

```
        }
    </SCRIPT>
    </HEAD>
    </BODY>
    </HTML>
```

If you entered the code properly you should see a series of images like these:

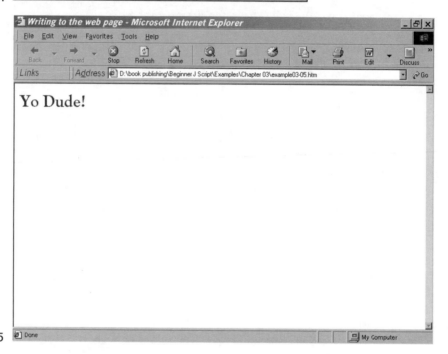

Figure 3-4

Figure 3-5

In this example we take the input of the user from a prompt box and then we type actual HTML code into the existing web page. You can use the document.write() method to type any valid HTML code. This allows you to alter the actual HTML content of your page based on the user's input. Now I want you to take just a moment to consider this. You can easily customize your web page based on a user's input. Again, let me stress that you can write any valid HTML code with this method. It may be a very simple technique, but in my opinion it's one of the coolest techniques.

## Antique Bookstore Project

Now we need to find a way to incorporate this script into our ongoing antique bookstore page. The following code provides the source for the antique bookstore page (at least the beginnings of it) and incorporates alerts and prompt boxes.

```
main.htm
<HTML>
<HEAD>
    <TITLE>Ye Olde Book Shoppe</TITLE>
<SCRIPT LANGUAGE="JavaScript">
<!--
var name = prompt("Please Enter your name:", "John Doe")
var message = "Click OK if you are using Netscape 5.0 or above, or Internet
Explorer 5.0 or above"
if (!confirm(message))
{
        alert("Please download the latest version of Netscape or Internet
Explorer.")
}
else
{
        alert ("Hello " + name )
}
// -->
</SCRIPT>
</HEAD>
<BODY BGCOLOR= White>
<CENTER>
<P><TABLE BORDER=1 CELLSPACING=0 CELLPADDING=0>
   <TR>
      <TD>
         <P><IMG SRC="gargshelf.gif" >
      <TD>
         <P><CENTER>Ye Olde Book Shoppe</CENTER>
     <TD>
         <P><IMG SRC="gargshelf.gif" >
</TABLE>
</CENTER>
<P>
</BODY>
</HTML>
```

We will put this into the main.htm page, thus giving a greeting when the user first loads the page.

## Summary

This chapter showed you how to give the user feedback using alerts and how to get information from the user using prompt boxes. It also showed you how to write directly to the HTML document. These simple techniques provide the groundwork for your expanding knowledge of JavaScript. These scripts also provide some basic user interaction with your web site. Pay particular attention to the document object, as you will see it in many places throughout this book.

# Chapter 4

# Image Effects

One of the most useful aspects of JavaScript is that it makes it quite easy for you to work with images. You can do a number of fascinating things with images in JavaScript. Some of the image techniques we will discuss in this chapter are merely fascinating "eye candy" to add to your web site. Others have a much more practical value.

## The Image Object

JavaScript has a built-in object called Image. We will be using this object in most of the scripts in this chapter. The Image object allows you to create objects that represent images of any type you could place in an HTML page (.JPG, .GIF, .BMP). To create an image object you simply create a variable as the Image type, like this:

```
var myimage = new Image()
```

The Image object has some properties you will need to use. The most important is the src property. This designates the actual image file you will use as a source for your Image object. The syntax for using this property is:

```
imageName.src = "myimage.gif"
```

The Image object can only be used to work with images already placed into the HTML page. You cannot add new images or completely delete images. You can, however, replace images with other images. This technique is best illustrated in what is commonly called a rollover.

# Rollover

The rollover is one of the most commonly used JavaScript imaging techniques. The essential purpose of the rollover is quite simple. When you use an image as an link, you can use the rollover method to cause that image to change when your mouse moves over it.

Let's assume your web page has an image on it that is used as a link to another page. What we want to accomplish is to have that image change when the user moves the mouse over the image. Below is an example of how to do this:

```
if(document.images)
{
    image1 = new Image
    image2 = new Image
    image1.src = "mysecondimage.gif"
    image2.src = "myfirstimage.gif"
}
else
{
    image1=""
    image2= ""
}
</SCRIPT>
```

Below is the code you put in your HTML body wherever you wish the link/rollover to appear.

**Example 4-1**

```
<A HREF ="nextpage.htm"
    onMouseover = "document.pic.src =image1.src"
    onMouseout = "document.pic.src =image2.src">

<IMG SRC = "myfirstimage.gif" name = "pic">

</A>
```

If you entered all the code properly you should observe something like this:

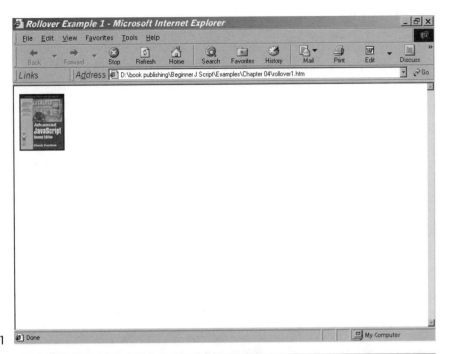

Figure 4-1

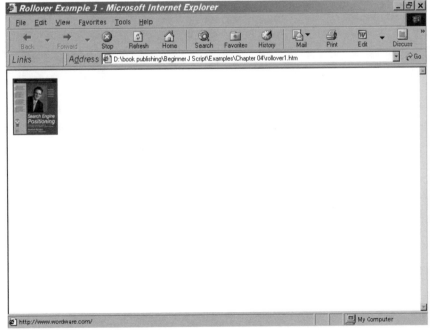

Figure 4-2

Let's examine this code for a moment. What the JavaScript is doing is creating variables that are instances of the Image object. Then we are setting the src property (the source) for those image objects, equal to some picture on your hard drive. When the web page first loads, the link will initially display "myfirstimage.gif". The space where that image is located, we have named "pic". When the mouse moves over the image/link we change the image space named pic, to contain the image in image1. When we move the mouse out of the image, we change it back to the picture in image2. The document keyword is a new keyword for you. It refers to the current HTML document that is loaded in the browser. This keyword will become even more important in later chapters.

## Slide Show

JavaScript allows you to create a fascinating slide show. Basically a single image is initially displayed and the user can scroll back and forth between different images. This is an outstanding feature to add to any e-commerce site. It allows your web site visitors to view all of your products, without cluttering the web page with dozens of images at one time. Let's look at a sample of how to do this:

**Example 4-2**

```
<HTML>
<HEAD>
  <TITLE>Slideshow Sample</TITLE>
  <SCRIPT LANGUAGE="JAVASCRIPT" >
      PicArray = new Array("pic1.jpg","pic2.jpg","pic3.jpg")
      CurrentPic = 0
      ImageCount = PicArray.length - 1
      function MovePrevious()
      {
            if (document.images && CurrentPic > 0)
            {
                    CurrentPic--
                    document.myPicture.src=PicArray[CurrentPic]
            }
      }
      function MoveNext()
      {
            if (document.images && CurrentPic < ImageCount )
            {
                    CurrentPic++
                    document.myPicture.src=PicArray[CurrentPic]
            }
```

```
        }

    </SCRIPT>
    </HEAD>
    <BODY BGCOLOR="WHITE">
    <CENTER>
    <H1>My Slide Show</H1>
    <IMG SRC="pic1.jpg" NAME="myPicture" ALT="My First Slideshow">
    <BR>

    <A HREF="javascript:MovePrevious()">&lt;&lt;  Move Previous</A>
    <A HREF="javascript:MoveNext()">Move Next &gt;&gt;</A>
    </CENTER>
    </BODY>
    </HTML>
```

Let's take a closer look at this script and see what is going on here. To begin with, in our JavaScript we are defining some variables:

```
        PicArray = new Array("pic1.jpg","pic2.jpg","pic3.jpg")
        CurrentPic = 0
        ImageCount = PicArray.length — 1
```

The first variable, PicArray, is simply an array of images. The second is a number indicating what element in the array we are currently looking at. All arrays start with zero so we initialize CurrentPic to 0. ImageCount is simply a number telling us how many images we currently have.

The next thing we do in this particular script is to define two functions, MovePrevious() and MoveNext(). The purpose of these functions is fairly obvious, to move forward or backward through the slide show. In each of these functions we have an if statement that simply asks two questions: Does this web page/browser support the image object (if document.Images) and are we already at the limit of our slide show (if you are at the beginning, you cannot select Move Previous)? If both of these conditions are met, then execute the function.

 **NOTE:** The symbol && denotes a logical AND, that is, both values must be true for the operation to be true. The || is a logical OR, that is, only one of the values must be true for the operation to be true.

The MovePrevious function simply uses the decrement operator (– –) to reduce CurrentPic and then displays that particular image from the image

**4**

Chapter

array PicArray. The MoveNext function is identical except it uses the increment operator (++).

The code in the body of the HTML document is a standard HTML reference, but rather than being a reference to another web page or an e-mail address, it is a reference to a function in our JavaScript.

If you enter the code properly, you can view a series of images like the ones shown here.

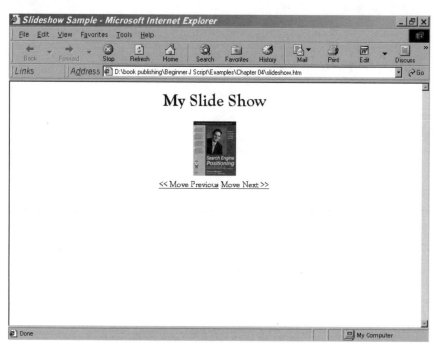

Figure 4-3

Figure 4-4

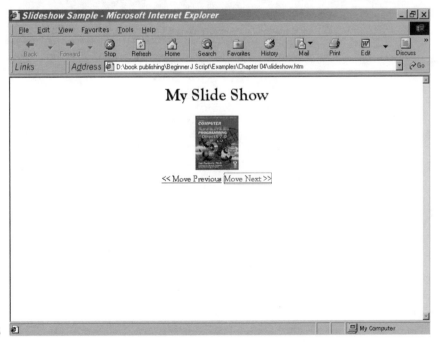

Figure 4-5

A slide show is a very practical piece of JavaScript that you will be able to use to enhance any site. However, it is ideally suited to presenting products for sale.

In our first slide show example we used links to call the JavaScript functions. You can also use buttons to create the same effect. All you need to do is replace the <A HREF> link section with code to place buttons on the screen. If you wish to do this, simply replace:

```
<A HREF="javascript:MovePrevious()">&lt;&lt; Move Previous</A>
<A HREF="javascript:MoveNext()">Move Next &gt;&gt;</A>
```

with:

```
<FORM>
    <INPUT TYPE="button" VALUE="<--" onClick="MovePrevious()">
    <INPUT TYPE ="button" VALUE ="-->" onClick="MoveNext()">
</FORM>
```

If you do this properly, it will produce the image you see here.

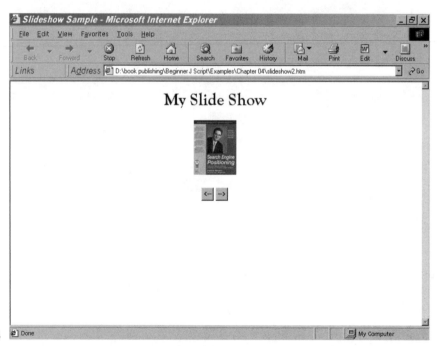

Figure 4-6

In case the HTML <FORM> tag is new to you, let's examine it. The <FORM> and </FORM> tags simply denote that what lies between them will be form elements. This is just like any of the other tags you have used before. INPUT TYPE tells the browser what type of form element to place on the web page. VALUE simply places a caption on the button you have created. onClick= simply says that when the button is clicked to do whatever comes after the equal sign. In our case it is a simple call to one of our JavaScript functions.

You could also use the <A HREF> link method we originally used, and instead of using words such as "move previous" you can use images. You simply replace the <A HREF> link section in the first slide show example with this:

```
<A HREF="javascript:MovePrevious()"><IMG SRC ="left.gif"</A>
<A HREF="javascript:MoveNext()"><IMG SRC ="right.gif"</A>
```

If you do this properly, it will generate an image like this:

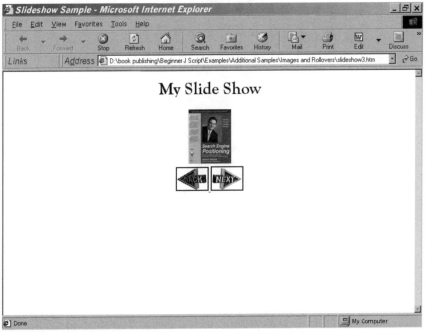

Figure 4-7

## Image Preview

Have you ever visited a web site that you felt was simply cluttered with too many images? I certainly have. One way to combat this is the slide show we just did. Another method is to initially display the images as small images, and allow the user to select which one they wish to view in full size. Here is a piece of code that will let you do just that.

**Example 4-3**

```
<HTML>
<HEAD>
  <TITLE> Image Preview
  </TITLE>

<SCRIPT LANGUAGE="JAVASCRIPT">
if (document.images)
{
   text1 = new Image
   text2 = new Image
   text3 = new Image
   text4 = new Image

   text1.src = "pic1.jpg"
   text2.src = "pic2.jpg"
   text3.src = "pic3.jpg"
   text4.src = "email2.gif"
}
else
{
   text1= ""
   text2 = ""
   text3 = ""
   text4 = ""
   document.textField = ""
}
</SCRIPT>
</HEAD>
<BODY BGCOLOR=white>
<TABLE>
    <TD>
    <A HREF="page1.htm" onMouseover="document.textField.src=text1.src">
        <IMG SRC="pic1.jpg"WIDTH = 25 HEIGHT = 25 ></A>
    <BR>
<A HREF="page2.htm" onMouseover="document.textField.src=text2.src">
        <IMG SRC="pic2.jpg"WIDTH = 25 HEIGHT = 25></A>
        <BR>
<A HREF="page3.htm" onMouseover="document.textField.src=text3.src">
        <IMG SRC="pic3.jpg"WIDTH = 25 HEIGHT = 25 ></A>
    <TD>
        <IMG SRC="doors.gif"  NAME="textField" ALT="Text Field">
</TABLE>
</BODY>
</HTML>
```

Let us examine this script and see what is happening. The first thing we see is the creation of some Image objects. We have seen this in previous scripts so it is really nothing new. In fact, the only thing really new about this script is that when the images are placed on the web page they are a very small size. Then when the mouseover event is fired, the image is displayed in full size to the right.

# Banner Ads

You have likely seen banner ads on web pages. It's actually pretty simple to do these in JavaScript. The following script takes three images and rotates through them at a given interval.

**Example 4-4**

```
<HTML>
<HEAD>
    <TITLE>Banner</TITLE>
    <SCRIPT LANGUAGE="JAVASCRIPT">
        ImageArray = new Array("banner1.gif","banner2.gif","banner3.gif")
        CurrentImage = 0
        ImageCount = ImageArray.length

        function RotateBanner()
        {
            if (document.images)
            {
                CurrentImage++
                if (CurrentImage ==ImageCount)
                {
                    CurrentImage = 0
                }
                document.Banner.src=ImageArray[CurrentImage]
                setTimeout("RotateBanner()", 5000)
            }
        }

    </SCRIPT>
</HEAD>
<BODY BGCOLOR="WHITE" onLoad="RotateBanner()">
<CENTER>
    <IMG SRC="banner1.gif"  NAME="Banner" ALT=" Banner">
</CENTER>
</BODY>
</HTML>
```

If you examine this script closely you will see that it is using techniques we have already seen but in a new way. So let's take a look at what is new in this script. To begin with, in the <BODY> tag you now see onLoad=RotateBanner(). This simply says to start our script when the page is initially loaded start our script. You will also notice this line in the script:

```
setTimeout("RotateBanner()", 5000)
```

This is using a built-in JavaScript function called Timeout. The number we pass it is in milliseconds. So we are telling it to timeout every five seconds. This causes it to load the next image every five seconds. You can play with the timing a bit. However, be careful: If the time is too short, no one will be able to actually read the banner ad.

# Image Pop-up

Another interesting technique you can use is to have an image pop up in a new window by itself when another image is clicked. Usually you will have a small version of the image, and when the user clicks on it they get the full image in a new window.

**Example 4-5**

```
<HTML>
<HEAD>
<TITLE>Example 04-05</TITLE>
<SCRIPT LANGUAGE="JavaScript" >
function newWindow(imagename)
{
     imageWindow = window.open(imagename, "imageWindow", width=320,height=240)
}
</SCRIPT>
</HEAD>
<BODY BGCOLOR="WHITE">
<H4>Double click on one of the following images to see the full size image</H4>
<IMG SRC="pic1.jpg" HEIGHT = 50 WIDTH = 50 onDblclick="newWindow('pic1.jpg')">

<IMG SRC="pic2.jpg" HEIGHT = 50 WIDTH = 50 onDblclick="newWindow('pic2.jpg')">

<IMG SRC="pic3.jpg" HEIGHT = 50 WIDTH = 50 onDblclick="newWindow('pic3.jpg')">
</BODY>
</HTML>
```

This code, if properly entered will produce an image like the following:

Figure 4-8

If you click on one of the images, it will pop up that image, full size, in a new window, as shown here:

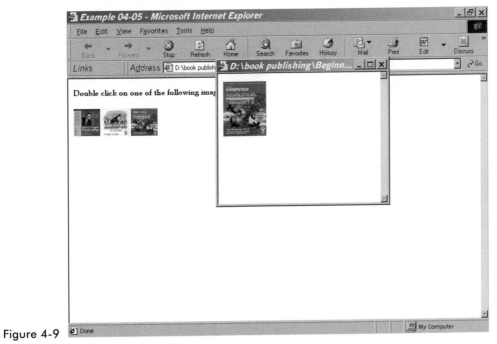

Figure 4-9

Let's take a look at this script and see what is happening. The actual script portion is actually quite simple. The function consists of a single line of code (it doesn't get much simpler than that!):

```
function newWindow(imagename)
{
    imageWindow = window.open(imagename, "imageWindow", "width=320,height=240)
}
```

Simply pass any image name to this function and it will launch a new window showing that picture. The way we open the new window is to use the open method of the window object. This method takes four required parameters and several optional ones. The first parameter tells it what to open. In our example it is an image, but you can open another HTML page as well. The second parameter gives JavaScript a name to refer to this new window by. Notice that this name matches the variable I chose. The next two parameters simply determine the height and width of the window. There are many more optional parameters, but they will be discussed in Chapter 6.

## Antique Bookstore Project

Now we can add some of these interesting techniques to our antique bookstore project. This will add some interesting features. First we are going to place a new web page in our project that uses the slide show to demo some books. This page is in the Antique Bookstore Project folder in the code files and is named books.htm. What I have done with that page is simply add in the slide show script, only I have used buttons to display the images.

```
<HTML>
<HEAD>
    <TITLE>Book Inventory</TITLE>
<SCRIPT LANGUAGE="JAVASCRIPT" >
    PicArray = new Array("book1.gif","book2.gif","book3.gif","book4.gif")
CurrentPic = 0
ImageCount = PicArray.length - 1
function MovePrevious()
{
    if (document.images && CurrentPic > 0)
    {
        CurrentPic--
        document.myPicture.src=PicArray[CurrentPic]
    }
}
```

```
            function MoveNext()
            {
                if (document.images && CurrentPic < ImageCount )
                {
                    CurrentPic++
                    document.myPicture.src=PicArray[CurrentPic]
                }
            }
        </SCRIPT>
        </HEAD>
        <BODY BGCOLOR = white >
        <P>
        <CENTER>
        <H2>This month's specials!</H2>
        <IMG SRC="book1.gif" HEIGHT=300 WIDTH =300 NAME="myPicture" ALT="Our Book
        Inventory">
            <FORM>
                <INPUT TYPE="button" VALUE="<--" onClick="MovePrevious()">
                <INPUT TYPE ="button" VALUE ="-->" onClick="MoveNext()">
            </FORM>
        </CENTER>
        </BODY>
        </HTML>
```

We also need to add a banner ad to the main.htm web page. For that I used a banner ad exactly like the one used earlier in this chapter. If you have been following along with all the examples, you should be starting to see a very interesting web site take shape.

## Summary

In this chapter you have learned how to use various image modification scripts to create a variety of interesting visual effects. It is important that you actually try each of these scripts before moving on. The principles you learn here will be carried throughout the book. You will also find that the interesting visual effects are the items most demanded by users.

**4**

Chapter

# Background Effects

Web page backgrounds can be somewhat dull. Even if you use an image as the background, it still is static. With JavaScript you can perform a number of interesting effects with the background. Each of these effects will add a great deal of visual impact to your web site.

## Document Object

You were introduced to the document object in the last chapter. Recall that the document object represents the web page currently loaded into the browser. Using this object we can make changes to that document. Two properties of the document object that we will explore in this chapter are bgcolor and background. These properties are exactly like the tags in HTML. The bgcolor property sets the background color of the web page, and the background property sets an image as the background.

## Changing the Background Color

The first script we will examine simply changes the background color to match the color described in a link that the user passes their mouse over. Let's look at that script now:

**Example 5-1**

```
<HTML>
<HEAD>
    <TITLE>Color Changer</TITLE>
</HEAD>
 <BODY>
<CENTER>
    <A HREF="/"onmouseover="document.bgColor='blue'">Blue</A>
    <A HREF="/"onmouseover="document.bgColor='royalblue'">Royal Blue</A>
```

```
            <A HREF="/"onmouseover="document.bgColor='green'">Green</A>
            <A HREF="/"onmouseover="document.bgColor='red'">Red</A><BR>
            <A HREF="/"onmouseover="document.bgColor='magenta'">Magenta</A>
            <A HREF="/"onmouseover="document.bgColor='pink'">Pink</A>
            <A HREF="/"onmouseover="document.bgColor='purple'">Purple</A><BR>
            <A HREF="/"onmouseover="document.bgColor='Skyblue'">Light Blue</A>
            <A HREF="/"onmouseover="document.bgColor='yellow'">Yellow</A>
            <A HREF="/"onmouseover="document.bgColor='brown'">Brown</A>
            <A HREF="/"onmouseover="document.bgColor='white'">White</A><BR>
            <A HREF="/"onmouseover="document.bgColor='black'">Black</A>
            <A HREF="/"onmouseover="document.bgColor='coral'">Coral</A>
            <A HREF="/"onmouseover="document.bgColor='orange'">Orange</A>
        </CENTER>
        </BODY>
        </HTML>
```

In this example we simply set up a standard link where the word displayed is the name of the color we will use as the background color of the web page. When the page first loads, it will look like Figure 5-1.

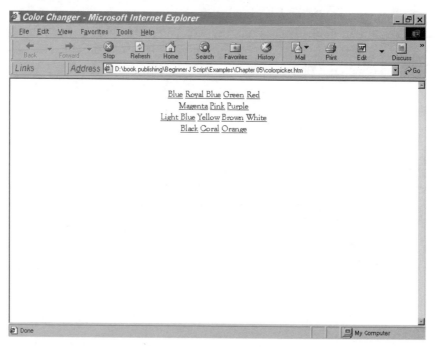

Figure 5-1

If you move your mouse over the word "black," the image will then look like Figure 5-2:

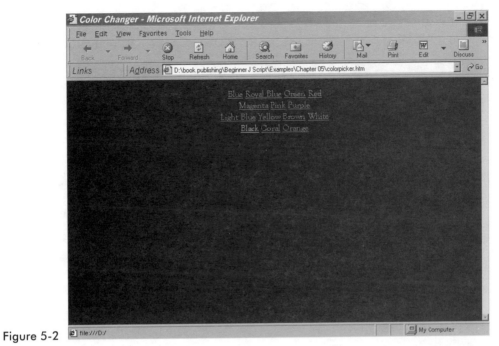

Figure 5-2

And then if you move it over the word "purple," it will look like Figure 5-3:

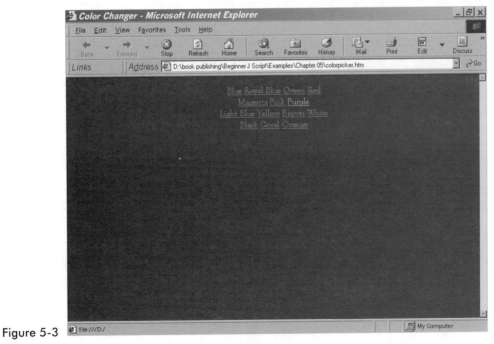

Figure 5-3

Now that you have seen this script in action, let's examine what is happening in the code itself. Each one of the separate links is constructed the same way.

```
<A HREF="/"onmouseover="document.bgColor='yellow'">Yellow</A>
```

The <a href= portion should be familiar to you since it is a standard hypertext reference, also known as a link. In this case, however, rather than linking to another web page or to an e-mail address, this simply links to itself. So when a mouse moves over the link we have established that the document object is used to set the background color of the web page to the desired color. This script is relatively straightforward but it's also an excellent way to begin to see the usefulness of the document object.

With this particular script or with variations thereof, you can change the color of the web page document any time you wish. Some variations to consider would be to change the background color based on the day of the week, time of day, or any other criteria you might wish. The only caveat is that you should ensure that the background color you use does not make it difficult to view the text on your web site.

## Changing the Background Image

Next I will show you how to use a technique very similar to the one used in Example 5-1 to change the image used in the background of your web page, rather than simply changing the color.

**Example 5-2**

```
<HTML>
<HEAD>
<TITLE>Example 05-02</TITLE>
<SCRIPT LANGUAGE="JavaScript">
    if (navigator.appName == "Microsoft Internet Explorer")
    {
        image1 = new Image()
        image2 = new Image()
        image3 = new Image()
        image4 = new Image()

        image1.src = "back1.gif"
        image2.src = "back2.gif"
        image3.src = "back3.jpg"
        image4.src = "back4.jpg"
    }
```

```
function changepicture(imgname)
   {
   if (navigator.appName == "Microsoft Internet Explorer")
   {
        document.body.background = eval(imgname + ".src");
   }
}

</SCRIPT>
</HEAD>
<BODY>
<CENTER>
[<A HREF="#" onMouseOver="changepicture('image1');">Marble</A>]
[<A HREF="#" onMouseOver="changepicture('image2');">Blue Marble</A>]
[<A HREF="#" onMouseOver="changepicture('image3');">Slate</A>]
[<A HREF="#" onMouseOver="changepicture('image4');">Dark Marble</A>]
</CENTER>
</BODY>
</HTML>
```

If you enter this code as you see it (and use the images found in the code files), you will get an image such as the one in Figure 5-4:

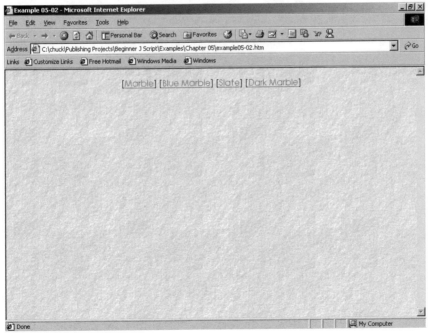

Figure 5-4

Then moving your mouse over the Marble link will give you an image like the one in Figure 5-5:

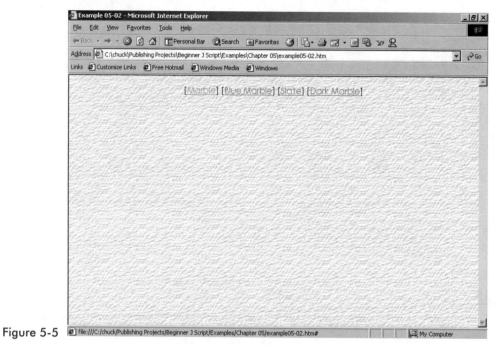

Figure 5-5

Moving the mouse over the Blue Marble link will show you an image such as the one in Figure 5-6:

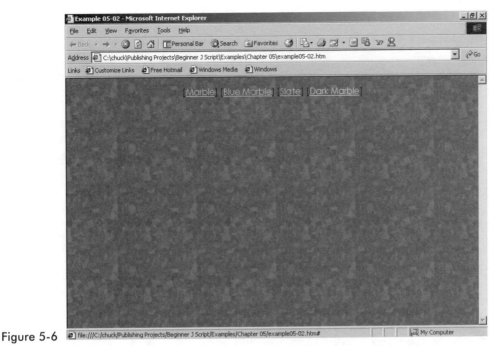

Figure 5-6

Let's take a moment to review the actual code here and make sure that you understand what is happening.

Note that the first line of the script finds out if the browser being used is Internet Explorer. This particular script will not work quite the same in Netscape. We will see in Chapter 6 that detecting the browser and working with it is very important.

```
if (navigator.appName == "Microsoft Internet Explorer")
```

This also introduces you to the navigator object, which allows you to determine a lot about the browser the person visiting your web site is using. Now assuming that it is Internet Explorer, we then proceed to create instances of the image object and set them to particular images we wish to use for our backgrounds. This code is virtually identical to the rollover code you saw in Chapter 4.

Let's look at another method for changing the background image. In the following example, when the user passes the mouse over a particular image that image becomes the background image for the web page.

5

Chapter

**Example 5-3**

```
<HTML>
<HEAD>
  <TITLE>Background Changer</TITLE>
 <HEAD>
<SCRIPT LANGUAGE="JavaScript">
if (navigator.appName == "Microsoft Internet Explorer")
{
   image1 = new Image()
   image2 = new Image()
   image3 = new Image()
   image4 = new Image()

   image1.src = "back1.gif"
   image2.src="back2.gif"
   image3.src = "back3.jpg"
   image4.src = "back4.jpg"
}
function changepicture(imgname)
{
if (navigator.appName == "Microsoft Internet Explorer")
   {
       document.body.background = eval(imgname + ".src");
   }
}
</SCRIPT>
</HEAD>
<BODY BACKGROUND="back1.gif">
   <A HREF="#" onMouseOver="changepicture('image1');"><img src="back1.gif"></A>
   <A HREF="#" onMouseOver="changepicture('image2');" ><img src="back2.gif"></A>
   <A HREF="#" onMouseOver="changepicture('image3');" ><img src="back3.jpg"></A>
   <A HREF="#" onMouseOver="changepicture('image4');""><img src="back4.jpg"></A>
</BODY>
</HTML>
```

This script works very much like Example 5-2, the only difference being that rather than using text links to the image, it uses an actual picture. When the user passes the mouse over the image, that image becomes the background image for the page. If you write the code correctly, you will get something like Figure 5-7:

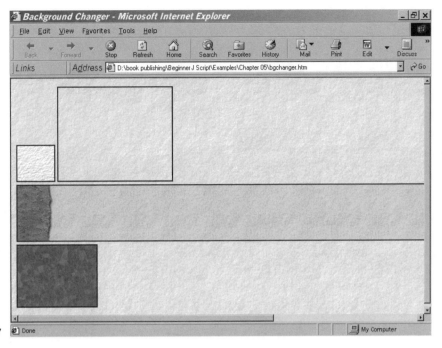

Figure 5-7

Then when you move your mouse over one of the images you will get something like Figure 5-8:

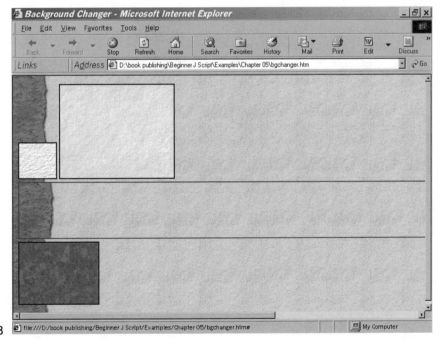

Figure 5-8

This example, much like the previous one (changing the background color) is more important for the principle it demonstrates. It is possible for you to use a different background image based on the date, time, or any other criteria you wish to use. In Chapter 7, "Working with Data and Time" I will show you an example of this.

## More Background Effects

In addition to changing the background colors and images, you can use JavaScript to make the background behave in interesting ways. One of the easiest effects to implement is the scrolling background. The following example shows a background that will scroll.

 **NOTE:** This works best with images that are uniform, such as rock textures, stars, lava, etc.

**Example 5-4**

```
<HTML>
<HEAD>
   <TITLE>Background Scroller</TITLE>
</HEAD>

<BODY>
<BODY BACKGROUND="back1.gif">
<SCRIPT LANGUAGE="JavaScript">
   var bgOffset = 0
   var bgObject = eval('document.body')
   function scrollbackground(maxSize)
   {
      bgOffset = bgOffset + 1
      if (bgOffset > maxSize)
            bgOffset = 0

      bgObject.style.backgroundPosition = "0 " + bgOffset;
   }
var scrtimer = window.setInterval("scrollbackground(50)",50)
</SCRIPT>
</BODY>
</HTML>
```

Now let's examine this particular script and see how it works. The first part of the script simply declares two variables:

```
var bgOffset = 0
var bgObject = eval('document.body')
```

The first variable, bgOffset, is simply an integer representing the number by which to offset the background image's position. The second variable, bgObject, represents the body of the document (notice that again we are finding uses for the document object).

Next we have the actual function that will do the scrolling of the background:

```
function scrollbackground(maxSize)
{
    bgOffset++
    if (bgOffset > maxSize)
            bgOffset = 0

    bgObject.style.backgroundPosition = "0 " + bgOffset;
}
```

Some integer value is passed to this function as maxSize. The first statement in the function simply increments bgOffset by 1. Then there is an if statement that checks to see if bgOffset has exceeded maxSize. If so, then bgOffset is reset to zero. We then simply set the background image position equal to the offset. What this will cause the background image to do is to shift down repeatedly until maxSize is reached, and then go back to the starting position. The larger the maxSize used, the less frequently the image will "pop" back up to the top, thus providing the person viewing your web page with a more fluid looking background.

Finally we come to the statement that calls the scrollBackground function:

```
var scrtimer = window.setInterval("scrollbackground(50)",50)
```

In this statement a variable is declared. That variable is set equal to the window object's setInterval function. Remember that the window object refers to the browser itself. Inside the setInterval function we call the scrollbackground function and pass it a max value. What also happens here is that a number is provided that indicates how frequently the shifting will occur. The lower this second number is, the faster the image will scroll.

This is perhaps, in my view at least, the most interesting background effect in this chapter. Provided it is used judiciously, it can add a dimension to your web site not otherwise obtainable. The primary issue to consider is what image you use. Remember that the image is not actually scrolling. We are simply creating the illusion of scrolling by shifting the image progressively further down, then bringing it back to the top. Because of this, an image with a homogenous background will look like a scrolling background. Images such as stars, water, clouds, stone textures, etc., work great for this.

## Antique Bookstore Project

Now let's add some of these techniques to our antique bookstore project and see how that works. The first thing we are going to include is a scrolling background on the main page. So let's look at the source code for that page (as it stands so far).

```
<HTML>
<HEAD>
    <TITLE>Ye Olde Book Shoppe</TITLE>
    <SCRIPT LANGUAGE="JAVASCRIPT">
        ImageArray = new Array("banner1.gif","banner2.gif","banner3.gif")
        CurrentImage = 0
        ImageCount = ImageArray.length
        function RotateBanner()
        {
            if (document.images)
            {
                CurrentImage++
                if (CurrentImage ==ImageCount)
                {
                    CurrentImage = 0
                }
                document.Banner.src=ImageArray[CurrentImage]
                setTimeout("RotateBanner()",3000)
            }
        }

    </SCRIPT>
</HEAD>
<BODY background="bod-bg.gif"  onLoad="RotateBanner()">
<CENTER>
<IMG SRC="banner1.gif"  NAME="Banner" >
<P><TABLE BORDER=1>
    <TR>
      <TD>
         <P><IMG SRC="gargshelf.gif">
      <TD>
         <P><CENTER>Ye Olde Book Shoppe</CENTER>
      <TD>
```

```
        <IMG SRC="gargshelf.gif">
</TABLE>
<P>
<P>
</CENTER>
<P>
</BODY>
</HTML>
```

We are going to add a second script to this page. This script goes in the body immediately after the <BODY background=> tag:

```
<SCRIPT LANGUAGE="JavaScript">
    var bgOffset = 0;
    var bgObject = eval('document.body');
    function scrollbackground(maxSize)
    {
       bgOffset = bgOffset + 1;
       if (bgOffset > maxSize)
               bgOffset = 0;
       bgObject.style.backgroundPosition = "0 " + bgOffset;
    }
    var scrtimer = window.setInterval("scrollbackground(50)",200);
</SCRIPT>
```

The background we are currently using is not particularly suited for scrolling so we will change that to a marble background. This will give us the following as our main.htm:

```
<HTML>
<HEAD>
    <TITLE>Ye Olde Book Shoppe</TITLE>

    <SCRIPT LANGUAGE="JAVASCRIPT">
        ImageArray = new Array("banner1.gif","banner2.gif","banner3.gif")
        CurrentImage = 0
        ImageCount = ImageArray.length
        function RotateBanner()
        {
            if (document.images)
            {
                CurrentImage++
                if (CurrentImage ==ImageCount)
                {
                    CurrentImage = 0
                }
                document.Banner.src=ImageArray[CurrentImage]
```

```
                    setTimeout("RotateBanner()",3000)
            }
        }
</SCRIPT>
</HEAD>
<BODY  background="back1.gif"  onLoad="RotateBanner()">
<SCRIPT LANGUAGE="JavaScript">
    var bgOffset = 0;
    var bgObject = eval('document.body');

    function scrollbackground(maxSize)
    {
        bgOffset = bgOffset + 1;
        if (bgOffset > maxSize)
                bgOffset = 0;

        bgObject.style.backgroundPosition = "0 " + bgOffset;
    }
var scrtimer = window.setInterval("scrollbackground(50)",50);
</SCRIPT>
<CENTER>
<IMG SRC="banner1.gif"  NAME="Banner" >
<P><TABLE BORDER=1>
    <TR>
      <TD>
          <P><IMG SRC="gargshelf.gif">
      <TD>
          <P><CENTER>Ye Olde Book Shoppe</CENTER>
      <TD>
          <IMG SRC="gargshelf.gif">

</TABLE>

<P>
<P>
</CENTER>
<P>
</BODY>
</HTML>
```

This code, if entered properly, should produce the following image:

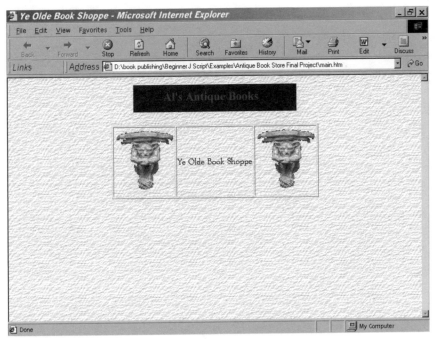

Figure 5-9

## Summary

This chapter has introduced you to some simple ways that you can manipulate the background color or image of a web page using JavaScript. Not only have you learned a fairly easy way to "jazz up" your web site, hopefully you have become more comfortable with JavaScript in general. One caution: Do not get carried away with background manipulation. A background that is too busy can be a distraction to site visitors.

Chapter 5

# Chapter 6

# The Document Object Model

With JavaScript you can perform lots of interaction with the browser. In fact, one of the more interesting things you can do with JavaScript is to detect the browser being used. You can then use the document objects to perform different operations. Remember from your previous chapters that the document object represents the web page that is currently loaded in the browser (i.e., the HTML document that the JavaScript is running in). The navigator object represents the browser being used. The window object represents the specific instance of the browser being used. You can easily have multiple instances of the browser open, viewing different web pages. We will look at each of these objects in detail in this chapter and explore ways to utilize them to enhance your web page.

 **NOTE:** Objects often consist of other objects. The term *nested objects* is usually used to characterize such child objects. The nested structure of an object is also known as its *hierarchy*. The highest-level object is the one that does not have any parent object. Browser objects are classic examples for hierarchy usage, because they are deeply nested. The browser object structure is fairly complex, so it is difficult to remember each and every property at the bottom of the tree. However, I will attempt to familiarize you with the basics of the browser object hierarchy.

## The window Object Hierarchy

The window object is the top-level object of the hierarchy. It contains properties that apply to the entire window. For example, the status bar of the browser is a property of this object. The window object has several properties we will look at.

The first is the status property. The window.status property represents the status bar at the bottom of your browser. You can use this property to display messages to the user in the status bar. We will examine some creative ways to use this a little later.

The window.alert, window.confirm, and window.prompt properties of the window object allow you to give messages to the user and receive feedback.

## document Object

By far the most useful property of the window object is the document object. It contains properties for the current page loaded in the window. With this object you can make all kinds of alterations to a web page. Almost everything in the page is a property of the document object, including links, images, forms and their elements, anchors, and more.

The document object itself has properties you can utilize. The URL property specifies the current URL of the web page. This is a read-only property. A closely related property is the document.location property. You can use this property to change to another location. That can be quite useful, and you will see it in several scripts.

The referrer property is also closely related to the URL and location properties. It represents the web page that the user was at just prior to loading the current page. This can be quite useful as we will see later on.

There are other properties that give you access to specific information about the web page you are in. The title property allows you to change the title of the document. The lastModified property allows you to see when this HTML document was last modified.

## history Object

The history object is also a property of the window object. It contains properties of the URLs the user has previously visited. This information is stored in a history list, and is accessible through the browser's menu. This object also contains methods enabling you to send the user's browser to a URL found in the history list.

The length property simply tracks the length of the history. It tells you how many items are listed in the history. The current property contains the value of the page you are currently in. For navigation you will use the next and previous properties, as they allow you to move forward and backward through the history.

All of these objects are linked together into a well-defined hierarchy referred to as the Document Object Model (DOM). Through creative use of the Document Object Model, you can do some very interesting things in JavaScript. But first you need to become acquainted with this model and what its elements do.

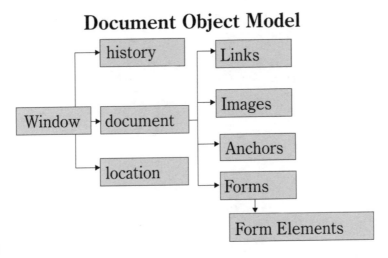

Figure 6-1

## The document Object

As previously noted, the document object represents the web page that the JavaScript is actually running in. Technically speaking, the document object is a property of the window object. We have previously used it to ensure that the web page will support the image object. In Chapter 4 we used if(document.images) in our scripts to make sure that the web page would support the image object. The document object has a variety of other fascinating methods. However, perhaps the easiest, but most versatile, method is the write method.

The write method literally allows you to write to the web page directly. For example, if you simply include this line of code:

```
Document.write("Howdy")
```

It will write the word "Howdy" to the web page. Now simply writing "Howdy" on a web page is not particularly interesting. A much more interesting application is to dynamically change the web page based on some criteria you choose.

6

Chapter

In the following example, we will ask the web page visitor to identify their gender and alter the appearance of the web page based on their answer.

**Example 6-1**

```
<HTML>
<HEAD>
   <TITLE>Gender Bender</TITLE>
<SCRIPT LANGUAGE="JavaScript">
var gender = prompt("Enter M for Male and F for female","F")
if(gender=="M")
{
   document.write('<BODY BGCOLOR = Blue>')
   document.write('<FONT COLOR = Red>')
   document.write('Yo Dude')
   document.write('</FONT>')
}
else
{
   document.write('<BODY BGCOLOR = Pink>')
   document.write('<FONT COLOR =Black>')
   document.write('You go girl')
   document.write('</FONT>')
}
</SCRIPT>
</HEAD>
<BODY>
</BODY>
</HTML>
```

This script is really quite simple. It simply asks the user to enter their gender and based on that information it proceeds to alter the properties of the HTML document. You can really expand upon this to have different background images, fonts, and even background music based on the information the user provides you. With our example, if you entered everything correctly, you should see a screen like the one shown here:

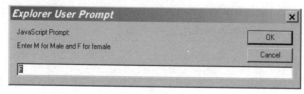

Figure 6-2

And then you will see one of the following screens, depending on how you answer the prompt shown in Figure 6-2:

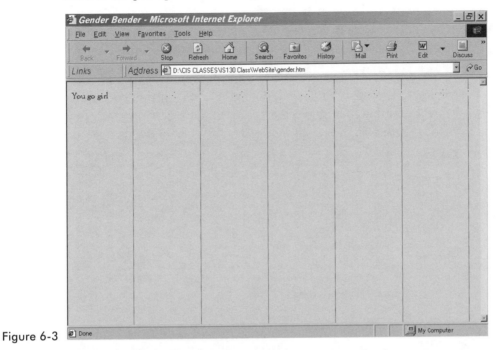

Figure 6-3

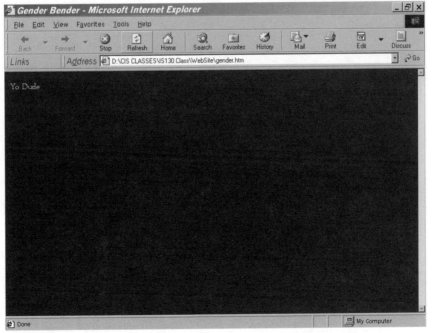

Figure 6-4

# The window Object

As I mentioned previously the window object represents the browser window in which the script is running. This particular object has some really interesting methods built in. We will explore some of them here.

One of the first things you can do with the window object is to open up other windows. The openWindow method was briefly introduced in Chapter 4, and we will examine it in more detail here. In the following example we open up a window with a picture displayed in it.

**Example 6-2**

```
<HTML>
<HEAD>
   <TITLE>Open a New Window</TITLE>
<SCRIPT LANGUAGE="JavaScript">
   function OpenWindow()
   {
      var NewWindow = window.open("advjscript.jpg", "NewWindow",
      "width=350,height=400")
   }
</SCRIPT>
</HEAD>
<BODY BGCOLOR=White>
<A HREF="javascript:OpenWindow()">Advanced Java Script</A>
</BODY>
</HTML>
```

The meat of this script is the single line of code found inside the openWindow function. The first parameter passed to this function is what you wish to open. This can be another HTML document or an image. The second parameter passed is the name of the variable that is going to represent this new window. In our case that is NewWindow. The last parameter is the height and width of the new window we are opening.

This script is fairly simple and easy to use. Even so, it can be very useful. For example, if you have a list of products on your web site and you do not wish to clutter the HTML document with all the details of every product, you can use this script to allow the user to view a page with those details when they click on the name of a product.

The only real problem with our example for launching a new window is that if the item you are launching is larger than the size parameters you give it, there aren't any scroll bars to let you see the whole image. The next example is very similar to the previous one, except that it adds something to the window.open method call to include scroll bars.

**Example 6-3**

```
<HTML>
<HEAD>
    <TITLE>Open a New Window</TITLE>
    <SCRIPT LANGUAGE="JavaScript">
    function OpenWindow()
    {
        var NewWindow = window.open("example06-03b.htm", "NewWindow",
                "width=350,height=200,scrollbars=yes")
    }
    </SCRIPT>
</HEAD>
<BODY BGCOLOR=White>
<A HREF="javascript:OpenWindow()">Advanced Java Script</A>
</BODY>
</HTML>
```

Simply adding scrollbars=yes right after the dimension parameters will give the new window you launch scroll bars! You can also add the line toolbar=yes so that your new window will have your browser's standard toolbar, if you wish.

The next example combines the scroll bars, the toolbars, and a method for the original window to close the window it launched.

**Example 6-4**

```
<HTML>
<HEAD>
    <TITLE>Close Windows</TITLE>
<SCRIPT LANGUAGE="JavaScript">
    var childwindow = null
    function opennewwindow()
    {
        childwindow = window.open("example06-03b.htm","childwindow",
            "width=300,height=200,toolbar=yes,scrollbars=yes,")
    }
    function closenewwindow()
    {
        if (childwindow && !childwindow.closed)
            {
                childwindow.close()
            }
```

```
        }
    </SCRIPT>
    </HEAD>
    <BODY BGCOLOR=White>
        <CENTER>
        <H3>
            <A HREF="javascript:opennewwindow()">View Advanced JavaScript</A>
            <BR>
            <A HREF="javascript:closenewwindow()">Close Advanced JavaScript</A>
        </H3>
        </CENTER>
    </BODY>
    </HTML>
```

The only real difference in this script is the closenewwindow function. In that function I simply use the name of the variable that represents the new window that was launched, and call the closewindow() method. Although this difference is small it is significant. Allowing the user to close the child window from the parent window that launched it is very important. If you entered the code properly you will see something like this image:

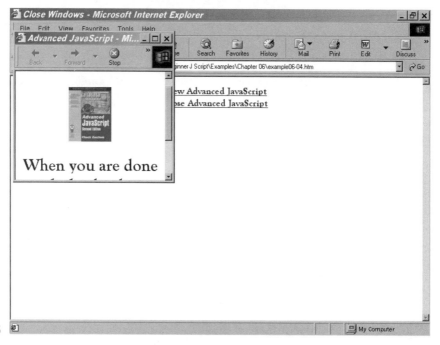

Figure 6-5

# The navigator Object

The navigator object represents the browser you are working with. From this object you can find the type of browser that is being used and the version number. Most scripts will run fine in either Microsoft Internet Explorer or Netscape Navigator. However, some scripts will not. It is a good idea, when using such scripts, to determine the browser that is being used before attempting to run a script.

The following example finds out what browser is being used and displays that information to the screen using the document object's write method.

**Example 6-5**

```
<HTML>
<HEAD>
    <TITLE>Browser Detection</TITLE>
</HEAD>
<BODY BGCOLOR=White>
<SCRIPT LANGUAGE="JavaScript">
var browsername= navigator.appName
var browserversion = navigator.appVersion
    if (browsername == "Microsoft Internet Explorer")
    {
        document.write("You are using MS Internet Explorer version " +
                browserversion)
    }
    else
    {
        document.write("You are using Netscape Navigator version " +
                browserversion)
    }
</SCRIPT>
</BODY>
</HTML>
```

This rather simple example illustrates some of the practical things you can do with the navigator object. If you entered the code properly you should see something like this:

**6**

Chapter

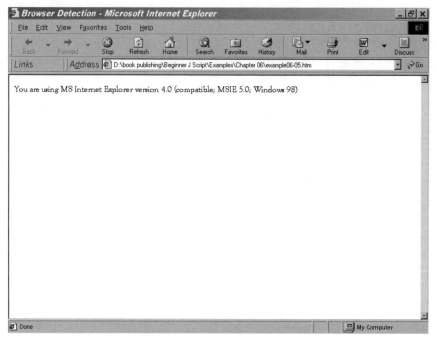

Figure 6-6

## Using the history Object

At the beginning of this chapter you were introduced to the history object. Now I will show you some examples of this object in use.

**Example 6-6**

```
<HTML>
<HEAD>
    <TITLE>Example 06-06.htm</TITLE>
</HEAD>

<SCRIPT LANGUAGE="JavaScript">
function goback()
{
    history.back()
}

function goforward()
{
    history.forward
}
</SCRIPT>
<BODY BGCOLOR=White>
```

```
<FORM>
      <INPUT TYPE ="button" VALUE ="Back" onClick="javascript:goback()">
      <INPUT TYPE ="button" VALUE ="Forward" onClick="javascript:
                  goforward()">
</FORM>
</BODY>
</HTML>
```

This rather simple example uses two JavaScript functions that each contain a single line of code. Each function uses the history object to move forward or backward in the document's history. These functions are called from HTML buttons on the body of the HTML document.

## Antique Bookstore Project

With each chapter in this book, not only will your skills grow but our antique bookstore project grows. So now let us take what we have learned in this chapter and add it to the antique bookstore. In this case we are going to add some pages describing some antique books. Since this is a fictitious bookstore, I am going to simply make up information about books.

We are going to add a new page named inventory.htm. This page will contain the latest additions to the bookstore's inventory. We will have to, of course, add a link on the tool.htm page. Also each book has a very simple page called inventory1.htm, inventory2.htm, etc., to display each of the books. This page simply has some text and a picture of the book. But now for the source code for the new page.

```
<HTML>
<HEAD>
    <TITLE>Book Inventory</TITLE>
<SCRIPT LANGUAGE="JAVASCRIPT" >
    var childwindow = null
        function openbook1()
        {
            childwindow = window.open("inventory1.htm","childwindow",
                    "width=400,height=400,scrollbars=yes")
        }
        function openbook2()
        {
            childwindow = window.open("inventory2.htm","childwindow",
                    "width=400,height=400,scrollbars=yes")
        }
        function openbook3()
```

**6**

Chapter

```
                {
                        childwindow = window.open("inventory3.htm","childwindow",
                                        "width=400,height=400,scrollbars=yes")
                }
                function openbook4()
                {
                        childwindow = window.open("inventory4.htm","childwindow",
                                        "width=400,height=400,scrollbars=yes")
                }
        </SCRIPT>
        </HEAD>
        <BODY   background="back1.gif" >
        <P>
        <CENTER>
                        <H2> This month's newest additions!
        </CENTER>

                        <P>
                        <A HREF="javascript:openbook1()">View Shakespeare</A><BR>
                        <A HREF="javascript:openbook2()">View Dickens</A><BR>
                        <A HREF="javascript:openbook3()">View Poe</A><BR>
                        <A HREF="javascript:openbook4()">View King James Bible</A><BR>
                        </H2>
        </BODY>
        </HTML>
```

What is most interesting about this web page is that we are using four different functions to load four different web pages. Other than that, this is the same basic launching of a new window that we saw earlier in our chapter, only applied to our antique bookstore!

## Summary

In this chapter you have been introduced to the document, window, and navigator windows. Hopefully you are beginning to get a feel for some of the fascinating features that JavaScript offers you through these built-in objects. I would also hope that at this point you are getting comfortable with JavaScript in general.

Some of the interesting things you have learned in this chapter include the ability to open up new windows, detect what type of browser is being used, and customize the actual HTML document based on any criteria you choose.

# Chapter 7

# Working with Date and Time

JavaScript makes it relatively easy to work with date and time data via its built-in Date object. With this object you can determine the current time, day of the week, and year. You can also change the time and date to any time or date you wish. As we move through this chapter you will see some interesting applications of the methods of this object.

## Time of Day

Rather than starting off with some tedious details about the methods and properties of the Date object, let us start with an easy-to-use but interesting script. In this script we determine the time of the day and give the visitor to our page a greeting based on that time of day. Let me point out that the Date method used here, getHours, returns the hours on a 24-hour clock. In other words, if it's 20 minutes after midnight, getHours will return a zero; if it's 6 P.M., getHours will return an 18.

### Example 7-1

```
<HTML>
<HEAD>
    <TITLE>Example 07-01</TITLE>
<SCRIPT LANGUAGE="JavaScript">
var mydate = new Date()
var mytime = mydate.getHours()
if (mytime<12)
    alert("Good Morning")
else
{
    if(mytime<17)
        alert("Good Afternoon")
    else
        alert("Good Evening")
```

87

```
    }
    </SCRIPT>
    </HEAD>
    <BODY>
    </BODY>
    </HTML>
```

This script is rather simple but it does illustrate the essentials of using the Date object. The first thing we do is create an instance of the Date object:

```
var mydate = new Date()
```

The next thing we do is create a variable to store the current time. Remember that this is the number of hours since midnight:

```
var mytime = mydate.getHours()
```

Now we have a simple if statement that checks what hour it is and, based on that time of day, gives an appropriate greeting. If you entered everything correctly, you should see something like the image here:

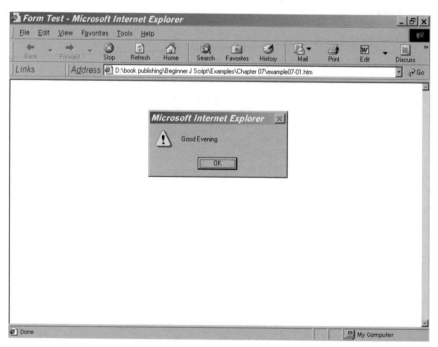

Figure 7-1

This script is fairly simple yet at the same time adds some interesting content to your web site. A simple time of day greeting can give your web site a personal touch and encourage more traffic (and web site traffic is the name of the game!).

## Day of Week

The next little script we will examine is one that gives a humorous greeting based on the day of the week. This script uses the getDay method of the date object. This method starts at zero for Sunday and then counts forward one by one.

**Example 7-2**

```
<HTML>
<HEAD>
     <TITLE>Example 07-02</TITLE>
<SCRIPT LANGUAGE="JavaScript">
var mydate = new Date()
var myday = mydate.getDay()
if(myday==0)
     alert("Sunday! Nap time!")
if (myday==1)
     alert("Another Monday...Arghhh!")

if(myday==2)
     alert("Tuesday...off to a slow week!")

if(myday==3)
     alert("Wednesday...Halfway home!!!")

if (myday==4)
     alert("just 1 more day! Hang in there!")

if (myday==5)
     alert("Thank God Its Friday!!!")
if (myday==6)
     alert("Saturday! Break out the BBQ!")
</SCRIPT>
</HEAD>
<BODY>
</BODY>
</HTML>
```

This script simply finds out what day it is and gives a humorous greeting appropriate to the day of the week. This should illustrate to you the getDay method, just as the previous example illustrates the use of the getHours method. If you entered it correctly, you should see something like the following image:

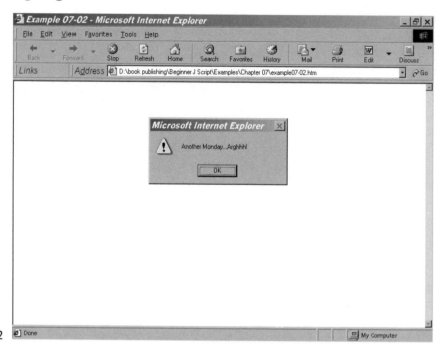

Figure 7-2

As you can probably guess, there are a number of methods for getting time and date information from the Date object. These are getYear, getHour, getDay, getTime, getMonth, getMinutes, and getSeconds. Each of these gives a particular output. The following table shows the output you can expect from each of these.

| Date Attribute | Range |
|---|---|
| seconds | 0-59 |
| minutes | 0-59 |
| hours | 0-23 |
| day | 0-6 |
| date | 1-31 |
| month | 0-11 |
| year | Note: In Netscape this is the years since 1900, while in Internet Explorer it's the actual year. So 2001 will show as 101 in Netscape and as 2001 in Internet Explorer. |

Now you can use these various methods to determine the current date, time, year, or other information. You can also change the date and time represented.

Now the first question most beginners ask is not how, but why would you want to. So let us look at an example where you might want to.

**Example 7-3**

```
<HTML>
<HEAD>
    <TITLE>Example 07-03</TITLE>
<SCRIPT LANGUAGE="JavaScript">

var year = prompt("What year where you born")
var month = prompt("What month where you born in")
var bday =prompt("What date where you born on")
var birthDay = new Date()
birthDay.setYear(year)
birthDay.setMonth(month)
birthDay.setDate(bday)
var day = birthDay.getDay()

if (day==0)
    alert("You were born on Sunday")

if (day==1)
    alert("You were born on Monday")

if (day==2)
    alert("You were born on Tuesday")

if (day==3)
    alert("You were born on Wednesday")

if (day==4)
    alert("You were born on Thursday")

if (day==5)
    alert("You were born on Friday")

if (day==6)
    alert("You were born on Saturday")

if (day==0)
    alert("You were born on Sunday")
</SCRIPT>
</HEAD>
<BODY>
</BODY>
</HTML>
```

Now take a close look at this script and let's discuss what it's doing. The first three lines simply prompt the user to enter the year, month, and day they were born. Note that these must be entered as numbers (i.e., September should be 9, October 10). The next four lines are where we see the code we are most interested in. Here we create a second Date object and set its year, month, and day to equal the values the user input. We then simply do a getDay() from this new Date object to find out what day of the week is produced.

# Setting Timeout

The setTimeout() method allows you to have some action occur after a given period of time has passed. The time is evaluated in milliseconds (i.e., 5,000 is 5 seconds). This can be a very useful function. Let's look at one example using the setTimout() method.

**Example 7-4**

```
<HTML>
<HEAD>
<TITLE>Example 07-04</TITLE>
<SCRIPT LANGUAGE="JavaScript">
function displayAlert()
{
    alert("5 seconds have elapsed since the button was clicked.")
}
</SCRIPT>
</HEAD>
<BODY>
<FORM>
Click the button for a reminder in 5 seconds.
<P>
<INPUT TYPE="button" VALUE="5-second reminder"
    NAME="remind_button"
    onClick="timerID = setTimeout('displayAlert()',5000)">
</FORM>
</BODY>
</HTML>
```

When you click the button, the event handler's script sets a timeout. The timeout specifies that after 5,000 milliseconds, or 5 seconds, the function displayAlert() is called. Therefore, 5 seconds after you click the button an alert box is displayed.

This is not a particularly exciting script but it does show you the use of a time-out. It is a relatively simple method to use, and is frequently used to simply create a pause between complex operations.

## Antique Bookstore Project

As with all the chapters in this book, once we have learned some new techniques we are going to add them to our antique bookstore project. We will simply add a day of week greeting to the main.htm page. But we are going to give it a more practical twist. Rather than give a humorous greeting for the day of the week, we will give the store hours for that day!

```
<HTML>
<HEAD>
        <TITLE>Ye Olde Book Shoppe</TITLE>
<SCRIPT LANGUAGE="JavaScript">
var mydate = new Date()


var myday = mydate.getDay()

if(myday==0)
        alert("Sunday- Sorry, we are closed today")

if (myday==1)
        alert("Monday- Sorry, we are closed today")

if(myday==2)
        alert("Tuesday- Our hours today are 10 a.m. to 6 p.m.")

if(myday==3)
        alert("Wednesday- Our hours today are 10 a.m. to 6 p.m.")

if (myday==4)
        alert("Thursday- Our hours today are 10 a.m. to 6 p.m.")

if (myday==5)
        alert("Friday- Our hours today are 10 a.m. to 7 p.m.")

if (myday==6)
        alert("Saturday- Our hours today are 10 a.m. to 4 p.m.")

</SCRIPT>
        <SCRIPT LANGUAGE="JAVASCRIPT">
```

```
                    ImageArray = new Array("banner1.gif","banner2.gif","banner3.gif")
                    CurrentImage = 0
                    ImageCount = ImageArray.length
                    function RotateBanner()
                    {
                        if (document.images)
                        {
                            CurrentImage++
                            if (CurrentImage ==ImageCount)
                            {
                                CurrentImage = 0
                            }
                            document.Banner.src=ImageArray[CurrentImage]
                            setTimeout("RotateBanner()",3000)
                        }
                    }
</SCRIPT>
</HEAD>
<BODY  background="back1.gif"  onLoad="RotateBanner()">

<SCRIPT LANGUAGE="JavaScript">
    var bgOffset = 0;
    var bgObject = eval('document.body');
    function scrollbackground(maxSize)
    {
        bgOffset = bgOffset + 1;

        if (bgOffset > maxSize)
            bgOffset = 0;
        bgObject.style.backgroundPosition = "0 " + bgOffset;
    }
var scrtimer = window.setInterval("scrollbackground(50)",50);
</SCRIPT>
<CENTER>

<IMG SRC="banner1.gif"  NAME="Banner" >
<P><TABLE BORDER=1>
   <TR>
     <TD>
        <P><IMG SRC="gargshelf.gif">
     <TD>
        <P><CENTER>Ye Olde Book Shoppe</CENTER>
     <TD>
        <IMG SRC="gargshelf.gif">
```

7

```
</TABLE>
<P>
<P>
</CENTER>
<P>
</BODY>
</HTML>
```

In my mind the most significant thing to notice about this web page is that we now have three JavaScripts all running on the same page. This is interesting because you will frequently want to run more than one script on a page.

## Summary

In this chapter you have seen how to use the Date object to accomplish a variety of date and time related tasks. You should be comfortable getting the current date, year, day, or time. You should also be comfortable setting the time and date using the setTime and setDate functions. I believe that you will find this particular information to be very practical for you while developing web sites.

# Chapter 8

# Working with Cookies

First we need to define what a cookie is (aside from a delicious snack, preferably with chocolate chips!). A *cookie* is simply a little bit of plain text data that your browser stores. This data concerns a particular web site. Your browser stores these cookies as unencrypted text files in a location specified by the browser. Once you learn to make cookies, you can have your web page store information concerning a visitor to your site. Then when they return to your site this information can be retrieved.

## Baking Your First Cookie

Cookies are not complicated but the code is lengthy. The only way to do this is to just jump right in. So I am going to show you the code for a cookie and then walk you through it explaining it line by line.

**Example 8-1**

```
<HTML>
<HEAD>
    <TITLE>Example 08-01</TITLE>
<SCRIPT LANGUAGE="JavaScript">
function setCookie(name, value, expires, path, domain, secure)
{
    var curCookie = name + "=" + escape(value) +
        ((expires) ? "; expires=" + expires.toGMTString() : "") +
    ((path) ? "; path=" + path : "") +((domain) ? "; domain=" + domain : "") +
    ((secure) ? "; secure" : "")
    document.cookie = curCookie
}
function getCookie(name)
{
    var prefix = name + "="
    var cookieStartIndex = document.cookie.indexOf(prefix)
```

```
        if (cookieStartIndex == -1)
        return null

        var cookieEndIndex = document.cookie.indexOf(";", cookieStartIndex+
                    prefix.length)

        if (cookieEndIndex == -1)
        cookieEndIndex = document.cookie.length

        return unescape(document.cookie.substring(cookieStartIndex +prefix.length,
            cookieEndIndex))
}
function deleteCookie(name, path, domain)
{
        if (getCookie(name))
        {
            document.cookie = name + "=" +((path) ? "; path=" + path : "") +
                    ((domain) ? "; domain=" + domain : "") +"; expires=Thu,
                    01-Jan-70 00:00:01 GMT"
        }
}

        var expiredate = new Date()
        expiredate.setTime(expiredate.getTime() + 31 * 24 * 60 * 60 * 1000)
        var name = getCookie("name")
        if (!name)
        {
            name = prompt("Please enter your name:", "John Doe")
            setCookie("name", name, expiredate)
        }

alert("Welcome back " + name)
</SCRIPT>
</HEAD>
<BODY BGCOLOR=White>
</BODY>
</HTML>
```

If you entered everything properly you should see something like this image:

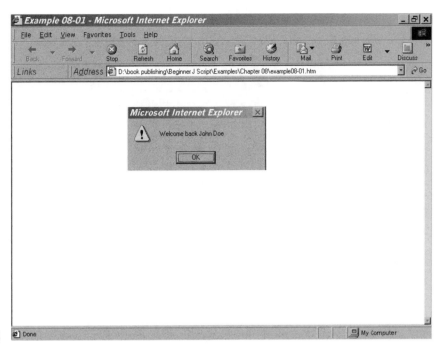

Figure 8-1

Now if you are beginning to panic at the sheer size of this particular script, please don't. It only looks convoluted. I will walk you through the source code line by line and together we will sort this out. Let us begin by looking at the first function you see, setCookie.

## setCookie

The syntax is:

```
function setCookie(name, value, expires, path, domain, secure)
```

First note that this function takes six parameters. Your code will only supply the first three. The last three are determined by the browser. The first parameter is called name. It is simply the name of the cookie.

It's a good idea to pick a name that is relevant to the type of data the cookie holds. The next parameter is the value or content that cookie will hold. We then have the expires parameter, which holds an expiration date for the cookie. If you do not set an expiration date, the cookie will expire the next time you reboot your PC. This is referred to as a *pre-expired cookie*.

Even though you don't supply the final three parameters it's a good idea to understand what they are. The fourth parameter simply is the path to where your browser stores cookies. The fifth parameter indicates what domain the cookies are associated with. A domain can have a maximum of 20 cookies. Finally we have the secure parameter, which simply tells us if this is a secure cookie or not.

Next the code simply creates a variable to contain the cookie information and concatenates it all together. Finally we use the document object's cookie property to add this cookie to the user's cookie list.

```
var curCookie = name + "=" + escape(value) +
    ((expires) ? "; expires=" + expires.toGMTString() : "") +
    ((path) ? "; path=" + path : "") +((domain) ? "; domain=" + domain : "") +
    ((secure) ? "; secure" : "")
    // Actually placing the cookie
    document.cookie = curCookie
```

What this function accomplishes is that it takes the values you pass it and the values that the browser itself passes it, and it creates a cookie to store that data.

### getCookie

The next function we examine is the code for the getCookie function. This is called to see if a valid cookie exists for this web page visitor. If it does, the function will simply return a null value. At that point you can prompt the user to enter the data, and then call setCookie(). However, if it does find a match, you can then use that data.

The function begins with this line of code:

```
var prefix = name + "="var cookieStartIndex = document.cookie.indexOf(prefix)
```

This code segment is creating a variable named prefix. That variable is set to equal the starting point, in the cookie file, of the cookie name that was passed to this function. This function will use the document object's cookie project to see if it can find this cookie. If it can, then it will return the index, and the cookie's value can be read in. If not, it will return a null. In fact, the very next line takes care of this:

```
if (cookieStartIndex == -1)
    return null
```

If cookieStartIndex cannot be found, simply have the function return a null, indicating that no cookie was found.

The next few lines try to find the ending point of this cookie. If one cannot be found, it is assumed that this is the last cookie your browser has in its cookie list and the end of this list is assumed to be the end of this cookie:

```
var cookieEndIndex = document.cookie.indexOf(";", cookieStartIndex+
                prefix.length)


  if (cookieEndIndex == -1)
      cookieEndIndex = document.cookie.length
```

Now once the function has determined that the cookie exists and that it has a start point as well as an ending point, then it's time to simply return the contents of that cookie. This is what the final line of the function accomplishes:

```
return unescape(document.cookie.substring(cookieStartIndex +prefix.length,
cookieEndIndex))
```

The third function, deleteCookie(), simply deletes a cookie if you pass it the cookie name. In the previous example this function was not actually called, but I thought I should show it to you in case you need it later.

## Calling the Functions

Now how do we actually use these functions to get cookies and to create them? Well, the last few lines of the script accomplish this, so let's give them a look. First, we have two lines of code that create a Date object and increment its value:

```
var expiredate = new Date()
expiredate.setTime(now.getTime() + 31 * 24 * 60 * 60 * 1000)
```

This expiredate object will be used to set the expiration date of our cookie. You can use the date functions to set this expiration date to any date you wish. I just picked this particular date for illustration purposes.

Now that we have an expiration date (and that will only be used when we set a new cookie, not when we get a cookie) we will now see if the cookie we want already exists on the web page visitor's machine.

```
var name = getCookie("name")
```

This code is really quite simple, but effective. We simply call the getCookie function and find out what it returns for the name cookie. If it finds a valid name, then we can simply use that name. If not, then we will get a null for a return value, in which case we can simply prompt the user to enter their name then use the setCookie function to create a cookie holding their name:

```
if (!name)
{
    name = prompt("Please enter your name:", "John Doe")
    setCookie("name", name, expiredate)
}
alert("Welcome back " + name)
```

And that, in a nutshell, is how our cookie script works. It is really not that complicated, it is simply long. So in order to make sure you do understand the concepts, let's examine another script that stores a somewhat different cookie.

## Bake Another Cookie

This cookie works similar to the previous one, and I hope that by examining both cookies you will get a good understanding of how cookies work. This script asks the user what background color they would prefer when viewing the web page, and saves that value in a cookie. Then anytime they visit the web page, it uses the background color they selected.

**Example 8-2**

```
<HTML>
<HEAD>
<TITLE>Example08-02</TITLE>
<HEAD>
<SCRIPT LANGUAGE = "JavaScript">
var expiredate= new Date();
expiredate.setTime(expiredate.getTime() + (30*24*60*60*1000))
var backcolor = getCookie("bgcolor")
if (backcolor == null)
{
    backcolor = prompt("What is your favorite background color?")
    setCookie("bgcolor", backcolor, expiredate)
}
document.bgColor=backcolor
function setCookie(name, value, expires, path, domain, secure)
{
    var curCookie = name + "=" + escape(value) +
        ((expires) ? "; expires=" + expires.toGMTString() : "") +
        ((path) ? "; path=" + path : "") +
        ((domain) ? "; domain=" + domain : "") +
        ((secure) ? "; secure" : "")
        document.cookie = curCookie
}
function getCookie(cookiename)
```

```
{
    var prefix = cookiename + "="
    var cookieStartIndex = document.cookie.indexOf(prefix)
        if (cookieStartIndex == -1)
            return null
        var cookieEndIndex = document.cookie.indexOf(";", cookieStartIndex+
                    prefix.length)
        if (cookieEndIndex == -1)
            cookieEndIndex = document.cookie.length

        return unescape(document.cookie.substring(cookieStartIndex
                    +prefix.length, cookieEndIndex))
}
</SCRIPT>
</HEAD>
<BODY>
</BODY>
</HTML>
```

If you entered the code properly, you should be able to see the following image in your browser:

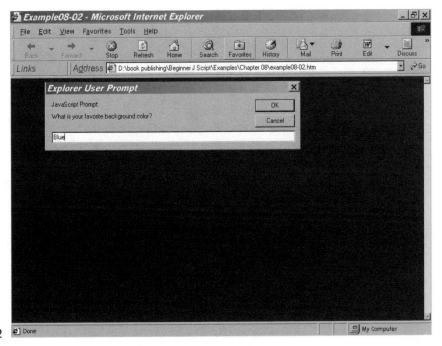

Figure 8-2

Hopefully you notice several similarities between this script and the last one. But let us go over this one together, just to make sure you understand everything that is happening. The first difference is merely structural. In this script I placed the call to the functions first, then the function definitions. This is the opposite of the order used in the previous script. I did this on purpose to show you that the order in which you do these actions really makes no difference.

Let's take a look at the first few lines of code and see what they are doing:

```
var expiredate= new Date();
expiredate.setTime(expiredate.getTime() + (30*24*60*60*1000))
var backcolor = getCookie("bgcolor")
```

First, we create a date object called expiredate. As you might guess, this is going to hold the expiration date for the cookie. We then set the expiration date for some time beyond the current time. Next, we call the getCookie function to retrieve the contents of the cookie named bgcolor. Whatever is returned is placed in the variable backcolor. If the cookie is found, then backcolor should contain some color. If no matching cookie is found, then we will get a null value in the variable backcolor.

Next we check to see if the value of backcolor is null. If so, we are going to prompt the user to enter their preferred color and then create a cookie to save that information. We will then set the background color of the current web page to the color the user has selected:

```
if (backcolor == null)
{
    backcolor = prompt("What is your favorite background color?")
    setCookie("bgcolor", backcolor, expiredate)
}
document.bgColor=backcolor
```

We do not need to closely examine the setCookie and getCookie functions because they are exactly identical to the ones used in the previous function. This illustrates a very important point. The process of creating a cookie, or retrieving one, is the same regardless of what you choose to name a cookie or what value you place in the cookie. This means you can use these same cookie scripts, with some minor alterations, to create cookies to save any data you might wish to save.

**NOTE:** The way a client's browser communicates with the web server is via HTTP (Hypertext Transfer Protocol). When a user requests a specific page, the browser sends that request to the web server. This activity is all transparent to the web page user. Among the items requested, an HTTP request includes a header that defines the most important attributes, such as the URL of the requested page. An HTTP request also includes the cookies.

The server then returns an HTTP response. This response also has a header that contains valuable information. The general structure of an HTTP header is as follows:

```
Field-name: Information
```

When the server returns an HTTP object to the client, it may also transmit some state information for the client to store as cookies. Since a cookie is basically simple text, the server-side script does not have the ability to abuse the client machine in any way. In addition to its textual value, a cookie contains several attributes, such as the range of URLs for which the cookie is valid. Any future HTTP requests from the client to one of the URLs in the above range will transmit back to the server the current cookie's value on the client.

An HTTP cookie is introduced to the client in an HTTP request using the following syntax:

```
Set-Cookie: NAME=VALUE; expires=DATE; path=pathName;
        domain=DOMAIN_NAME; secure
```

The attributes are as follows:

```
name=value
```

This simply specifies the name of the cookie and the value to be stored in the cookie. Technically, this is the only field that is required. All others are purely optional.

```
expires=date
```

As you probably guessed, this attribute simply sets an expiration date for the cookie. This field is optional. However, if no expiration date is set, a cookie will expire the next time the client machine is rebooted. The date string is formatted as follows:

```
Wdy, DD-Mon-YYYY HH:MM:SS
```

```
domain
```

The domain attribute makes sure that only hosts within the specified domain can set a cookie for the domain. Domains must have at least two or three periods, to avoid collision between domains of the form .com, .edu, etc. There are seven common top-level domains that require at least two periods in their domain name: com, edu, net, org, gov, mil, and int. All other domains require at least three periods in their domainName. An example of a domain name would be www.wordware.com.

The default value of domain is the host name of the server which generated the cookie response.

> *path=pathName*

Path specifies a subset of URLs in a domain for which a cookie is valid. Basically once you have found an appropriate domain, you have to find the individual web site within that domain that is relevant to this cookie.

> secure

If a cookie is marked secure, it will only be transmitted across a secured communication channel between the client and the host.

# Antique Bookstore Project

As you might guess, we are going to add this script to our antique bookstore project. We are going to use the first cookie script on the main.htm page of our project. This way we can retain the name of customers who visit our site and greet them when they return. As in each chapter, when we add something to a page in our project, I show you the complete code, including the previous code. This allows you to see the script in the context of the other HTML and other scripts already on the web page.

```
<HTML>
<HEAD>
    <TITLE>Ye Olde Book Shoppe</TITLE>
<SCRIPT LANGUAGE="JavaScript">
function setCookie(name, value, expires, path, domain, secure)
{
    var curCookie = name + "=" + escape(value) +
        ((expires) ? "; expires=" + expires.toGMTString() : "") +
        ((path) ? "; path=" + path : "") +
        ((domain) ? "; domain=" + domain : "") +
        ((secure) ? "; secure" : "")
        document.cookie = curCookie
}
function getCookie(name)
{
    var prefix = name + "="
```

```
        var cookieStartIndex = document.cookie.indexOf(prefix)
            if (cookieStartIndex == -1)
                 return null

            var cookieEndIndex = document.cookie.indexOf(";", cookieStartIndex+
                        prefix.length)

            if (cookieEndIndex == -1)
                 cookieEndIndex = document.cookie.length

            return unescape(document.cookie.substring(cookieStartIndex
                        +prefix.length, cookieEndIndex))
}

function deleteCookie(name, path, domain)
{
            if (getCookie(name))
            {
                 document.cookie = name + "=" +((path) ? "; path=" + path : "") +
                     ((domain) ? "; domain=" + domain : "") +"; expires=Thu,
                     01-Jan-70 00:00:01 GMT"
            }
}
        var expiredate= new Date()
        expiredate.setTime(expiredate.getTime() + 30 * 24 * 60 * 60 * 1000)
        var name = getCookie("name")
        if (!name)
        {
             name = prompt("Please enter your name:", "John Doe")
             setCookie("name", name, expiredate)
        }

alert("Welcome back " + name)
</SCRIPT>
<SCRIPT LANGUAGE="JavaScript">
var mydate = new Date()


var myday = mydate.getDay()

if(myday==0)
     alert("Sunday- Sorry, we are closed today")

if (myday==1)
     alert("Monday- Sorry, we are closed today")
```

```
if(myday==2)
    alert("Tuesday- Our hours today are 10 a.m. to 6 p.m.")

if(myday==3)
    alert("Wednesday- Our hours today are 10 a.m. to 6 p.m.")

if (myday==4)
    alert("Thursday- Our hours today are 10 a.m. to 6 p.m.")

if (myday==5)
    alert("Friday- Our hours today are 10 a.m. to 7 p.m.")

if (myday==6)
    alert("Saturday- Our hours today are 10 a.m. to 4 p.m.")

</SCRIPT>
    <SCRIPT LANGUAGE="JAVASCRIPT">
        ImageArray = new Array("banner1.gif","banner2.gif","banner3.gif")
        CurrentImage = 0
        ImageCount = ImageArray.length
        function RotateBanner()
        {
            if (document.images)
            {
                CurrentImage++
                if (CurrentImage ==ImageCount)
                {
                    CurrentImage = 0
                }
                document.Banner.src=ImageArray[CurrentImage]
                setTimeout("RotateBanner()",3000)
            }
        }


</SCRIPT>
</HEAD>
<BODY  background="back1.gif"  onLoad="RotateBanner()">

<SCRIPT LANGUAGE="JavaScript">
    var bgOffset = 0;
    var bgObject = eval('document.body');
    function scrollbackground(maxSize)
    {
        bgOffset = bgOffset + 1;
        if (bgOffset > maxSize)
```

8

Chapter

```
                    bgOffset = 0;
            bgObject.style.backgroundPosition = "0 " + bgOffset;
    }
var scrtimer = window.setInterval("scrollbackground(50)",50);
</SCRIPT>
<CENTER>
<IMG SRC="banner1.gif"  NAME="Banner" >
<P><TABLE BORDER=1>
    <TR>
        <TD>
            <P><IMG SRC="gargshelf.gif">
        <TD>
            <P><CENTER>Ye Olde Book Shoppe</CENTER>
        <TD>
            <IMG SRC="gargshelf.gif">
</TABLE>
<P>
<P>
</CENTER>
<P>
</BODY>
</HTML>
```

I hope you notice that we are now running five separate scripts on the same web page. Usually this would be discouraged, as it can make the web page appear too "busy." However, in this case it was done purposefully to illustrate a point. You can easily have multiple scripts on a single page. You simply need to place each script inside of its own <SCRIPT> </SCRIPT> tags.

## Summary

In this chapter you were shown a very useful application of JavaScript: cookies. Cookies are the most common way of retaining data about a web site visitor so that the data can be retrieved the next time the person visits that web site. This not only creates a more user-friendly web page, but it can save the user the trouble of having to re-enter key data every single time he or she visits the web site.

# Chapter 9

# Working with the Status Bar

The status bar is found at the bottom of the browser's window. Both Navigator and Internet Explorer have a status bar. It usually displays the current status of the document being loaded.

It can be useful for you to occasionally display information in the status bar. Fortunately this is very easy in JavaScript. In this chapter you will see a variety of ways you can display information in the status bar. Simply accessing the status property of the window object gives you access to the status bar.

## Image Data

One very easy technique is to display information in the status bar when a person passes the mouse over some image.

**Example 9-1**

```
<HTML>
<HEAD>
    <TITLE>Example 09-01</TITLE>
</HEAD>
<BODY BGCOLOR=white>
<CENTER>
<A HREF="somepage.htm"
    onMouseOver= " window.status='This is a link to some page'
    return true" onMouseOut="window.status= ' '
    return true">First Link</A> |

<A HREF="someotherpage.htm"
    onMouseOver="window.status='This is a link to some other page'
    return true"  onMouseOut="window.status='Please dont go '
    return true">Second Link </A>
```

```
</CENTER>
</BODY>
</HTML>
```

If you enter the code exactly as it appears above you should see the following images in your browser. When the page first loads you will see this:

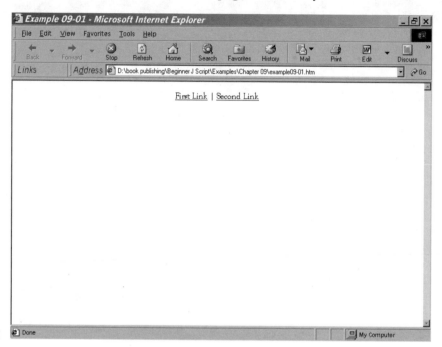

Figure 9-1

Then if you move your mouse over the first link, you will see a message in the status bar.

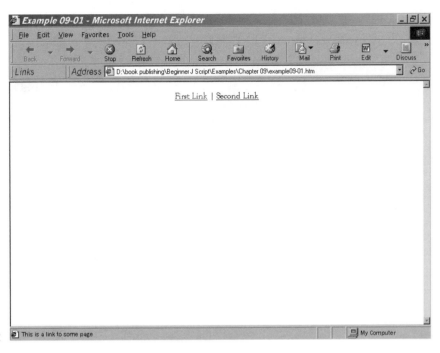

Figure 9-2

If you move your mouse over the second link, you will see a message in the status bar. With this link (unlike the first one) you will get another message when you move off of the link.

Figure 9-3

By closely examining the second link we can see clearly how this works. It begins with a standard HTML reference <A HREF="somepage.htm". But before we close the tag we have some other code.

The next line we see is onMouseOver=window.status='This is a link to some page'. What this is saying is simply that when a mouse moves over this link the text you see in the status bar of the browser should appear. An important thing to remember is that in your text you cannot have any apostrophes. Since the text itself is enclosed in apostrophes it will cause an error.

After this we have two choices for the onMouseOut event. We can simply write window.status="... as we did with the first link, or we can place some other text in the status bar when the mouse moves off of the link.

This particular little trick is not hard to use at all, and it adds an important dimension to your web site. Each of your links can now display more details in the status bar. This can be very useful for visitors to your site.

## T-Banners

The T-banner simulates a typewriter. It displays each message by typing it in, one character at a time. It seems as if someone is typing the message at a certain speed, deleting it upon completion. First, take a look at the script:

**Example 9-2**

```
<HTML>
<HEAD>
<TITLE>Example 09-02</TITLE>
<SCRIPT LANGUAGE="JavaScript">

var speed = 100  // this speed value actually works in reverse; lower the
                 // number to increase speed

var pause = 1000 // increase value to increase pause
// set initial values
var timerID = null
var bannerRunning = false
var offset = 0
var text = "How do you like this T-Banner"

function stopBanner()
{
```

```
        // if banner is currently running
        if (bannerRunning)
         // stop the banner
         clearTimeout(timerID)
         bannerRunning = false
}

function startBanner()
{
    stopBanner()
    showBanner()
}

function showBanner()
{


    if (offset < text.length)
    {
        var partialMessage = text.substring(0, offset + 1)
        // display partial message in status bar
        window.status = partialMessage
        // increment index of last character to be displayed
        offset++

        // recursive call after specified time
        timerID = setTimeout("showBanner()", speed)
        // banner is running
        bannerRunning = true
    }
    else
    {
        offset = 0
        timerID = setTimeout("showBanner()", pause)
        bannerRunning = true
    }
}
// -->
</SCRIPT>
</HEAD>
<BODY onLoad="startBanner()">
</BODY>
</HTML>
```

When you type in this script and run it in your browser, you should see something like the following:

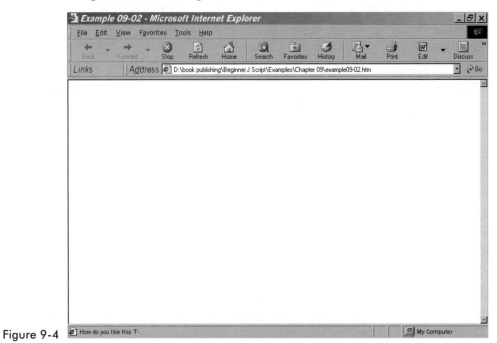

Figure 9-4

This script is actually rather simple. In fact, it is its simplicity that makes it work. The first portion of the script merely declares the variables that we will need throughout the rest of the script.

```
var speed = 100   // this speed value actually works in reverse; lower the
                  // number to increase speed
var pause = 1000 // increase value to increase pause
// set initial values
var timerID = null
var bannerRunning = false
var offset = 0
var text = "How do you like this T-Banner"
```

The first variable simply tells us how fast to put the banner in the status bar. The second tells us how much pause before running the banner again. The third variable is a timer variable that we initialize to a null value. The bannerRunning variable lets us track whether the banner is currently running or not. The offset variable is really key to the whole operation, as you will see shortly. The final variable is the text variable that simply contains whatever text we wish to display.

The stopBanner function merely causes the banner to stop displaying. The startBanner function ensures that the banner is not currently running (by calling the aforementioned stopBanner function), then calls the showBanner function. It is this last function with which we are concerned. It is here that the real action takes place in this script.

```
if (offset < text.length)
{
    var partialMessage = text.substring(0, offset + 1)
    // display partial message in status bar
    window.status = partialMessage
        offset++
    // recursive call after specified time
    timerID = setTimeout("showBanner()", speed)
    // banner is running
    bannerRunning = true
}
```

Let us examine this segment of script and make sure that you understand what it is doing. The offset variable, which you were introduced to previously, tells us which character in the text variable we are currently at. So the first thing we do is see if that value is still less than the length of the total text value. If it is then we execute the remaining code. The secret of the script is in just three lines:

```
    var partialMessage = text.substring(0, offset + 1)
    window.status = partialMessage
        offset++
```

What happens here is we grab the segment of the text variable from zero to the value of the offset + 1 and then we display that text in the status bar. On the first pass we will simply display the first character, then the second character, then the third, and so on. Although it appears that the characters are being typed across the status bar, what is really happening is that the status bar's value is completely changing each time to reflect a longer segment of the text!

After this, the function just keeps calling itself until the entire text is displayed. You should note that the process of having a function call itself is referred to as *recursion*. A function that does call itself is said to be a *recursive function*.

9

Chapter

## Antique Bookstore Project

As with all the chapters in this book, we now need to add some of what we have learned to our ongoing antique bookstore project. We are actually going to add two things. We will begin by using the first example I showed you to add some informational content to our inventory page.

*Inventory.htm*

```
<HTML>
<HEAD>
     <TITLE>Book Inventory</TITLE>
<SCRIPT LANGUAGE="JAVASCRIPT" >
var childwindow = null
function openbook1()
{
     childwindow = window.open("inventory1.htm","childwindow",
          "width=400,height=400,scrollbars=yes")
}
function openbook2()
{
     childwindow = window.open("inventory2.htm","childwindow",
          "width=400,height=400,scrollbars=yes")
}
function openbook3()
{
     childwindow = window.open("inventory3.htm","childwindow",
          "width=400,height=400,scrollbars=yes")
}
function openbook4()
{
     childwindow = window.open("inventory4.htm","childwindow",
          "width=400,height=400,scrollbars=yes")
}
</SCRIPT
</HEAD>
<BODY    background="back1.gif" >
<P>
<CENTER>
     <H2> This month's newest additions!
</CENTER>
<P>
<A HREF="javascript:openbook1()"
onMouseOver= " window.status='We have three copies of this book, all in fine
condition'
```

```
return true" onMouseOut="window.status= ' '
return true">View Shakespeare</A><BR>

<A HREF="javascript:openbook2()"
onMouseOver= " window.status='We just acquired this book last month'
return true" onMouseOut="window.status= ' '
return true">View Dickens</A><BR>

<A HREF="javascript:openbook3()"
onMouseOver= " window.status='This book is in fair condition'
return true" onMouseOut="window.status= ' '
return true">View Poe</A><BR>

<A HREF="javascript:openbook4()"
onMouseOver= " window.status='We have one copy in mint condition'
return true" onMouseOut="window.status= ' '
return true">View King James Bible</A><BR>
</H2>
</BODY>
</HTML>
```

## Summary

In this chapter you have seen that it is really quite easy to manipulate the status bar to display information. I have shown you a few direct examples to illustrate this point. You will find that the minimal effort required in implementing these techniques is well worth it. Your web site visitors will be able to get additional information in the status bar without you having to add unnecessary clutter to your web page.

# Chapter 10

# Creating Dynamic Menus

The visitors to your web site are probably used to desktop applications (running on their PC or Mac) that allow them to navigate the software via a wide range of menus. I am sure that you have used drop-down menus, pop-up menus, and other type of menus as well. Fortunately it is not particularly difficult to place such menus in your web page using JavaScript.

In order to create many of these menus we have to depend on a web technology called cascading style sheets. Since this book is about JavaScript we don't go into depth on exactly how cascading style sheets work; we just use them in conjunction with our standard HTML and JavaScript. It is entirely possible to use these scripts with only a very cursory knowledge of style sheets.

## Pop-Up Menus

The first menu type we will examine produces a simple pop-up menu when the user moves the mouse over a particular segment of text. Let us look at a sample and examine it to understand how it works.

**Example 10-1**

```
<HTML>
<HEAD>
    <TITLE>ex10-01</TITLE>
    <STYLE TYPE="text/css">
        .popup {border-width:4; border-style: solid; border-color:blue;
            position:absolute; background-color:yellow; visibility:hidden}
    </STYLE>
    <SCRIPT>
    function setUp()
    {
        makepopup ("Item1" ,280, "This is the popup for item 1")
        makepopup ("Item2",240, "Hey this is another popup.")
```

```
                    makepopup ("Item3",280, "Last, but not least, popup3.")
            }
        function makepopup (id, width, message)
        {
            var htmltext = '<STYLE
                TYPE="text/css">#'+id+'{width:'+width+';}</STYLE>';
                htmltext +='<DIV CLASS="popup" id="'+id+'">'+message+'</DIV>';
                document.write(htmltext);
        }

        function show(id, event)
        {
            document.all[id].style.pixelLeft = (document.body.scrollLeft
                    +event.clientX) + 10;
            document.all[id].style.pixelTop = (document.body.scrollTop +
                    event.clientY) + 10;
            document.all[id].style.visibility="visible";
        }


        function hide(id)
            {
                document.all[id].style.visibility="hidden";
            }


    </SCRIPT>
    </HEAD>
    <BODY BGCOLOR=white>
    <CENTER>
        List of Items
        <UL>
            <LI>
                <A HREF="" onMouseOver="show('Item1', event)"
                        onMouseOut="hide('Item1')">Item 1</A>
            <LI>
                <A HREF="" onMouseOver="show('Item2', event)"
                        onMouseOut="hide('Item2')">Item 2</A>
            <LI>
                <A HREF="" onMouseOver="show('Item3', event)"
                        onMouseOut="hide('Item3')">Item 3</A>
        </UL>

    <SCRIPT LANGUAGE="JavaScript">
        setUp()
    </SCRIPT>
```

```
</BODY>
</HTML>
```

This script may look a bit complicated but don't worry, it's not. The first new item you may notice is the <STYLE> tag. This is used with cascading style sheets (CSS) and we use it to create the little balloon. It is common to use these cascading style sheets in conjunction with a scripting language such as JavaScript. Essentially its parameters define the way in which the pop-up window will look. After that, the rest of the script is fairly standard JavaScript. Let's take a closer look

The first function you see, setUp, simply defines the parameters the pop-up menu will have. This includes what text it will display and its width. This function in turn uses makepopup to create the pop-up window with the parameters you put in setUp.

The function Show() actually displays the pop-up window. This function is called when the mouse moves over the text in the body of your HTML. The hide function simply hides the pop-up window and is called when the mouse moves off of the text in the body of your HTML. Both of these functions utilize elements of the cascading style sheet, particularly the visible property.

If you entered the code correctly, you should be able to use your browser to view something similar to the following:

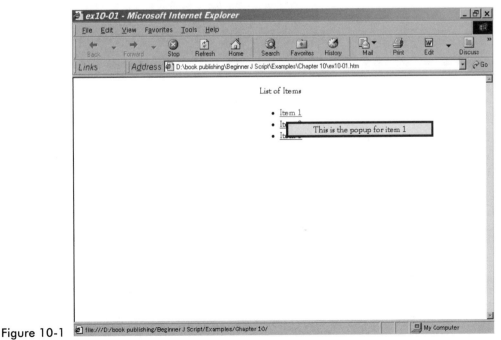

Figure 10-1

## Drop-Down Menus

The drop-down menu simply uses an HTML choice form element. This looks like a drop-down or combo box in Microsoft Windows. You use this form element to provide the user with a list of choices, then take their choice and pass it to your JavaScript. Let's look at an example.

**Example 10-2**

```
<HTML>
<HEAD>
<TITLE> Example 10-02</TITLE>
<SCRIPT LANGUAGE = "JavaScript">

function movetourl()
{
    window.location=document.dropmenu.website.options[document.dropmenu.
        website.selectedIndex].value
}
</SCRIPT>
</HEAD>
<BODY>
<FORM NAME="dropmenu">
    <SELECT NAME="website">
    <OPTION VALUE=""><B>Choose your link</b>
    <OPTION VALUE="http://www.wordware.com">WordWare
    <OPTION VALUE="http://www.amazon.com">Amazon Books
    <OPTION VALUE="http://www.nortexsolutions.com">Nortex Solutions
    </SELECT>
    <INPUT TYPE="button" VALUE="Go" onClick="movetourl()">
</FORM>
</BODY>
</HTML>
```

If you enter all the code correctly, you should be able to see something like the following illustration:

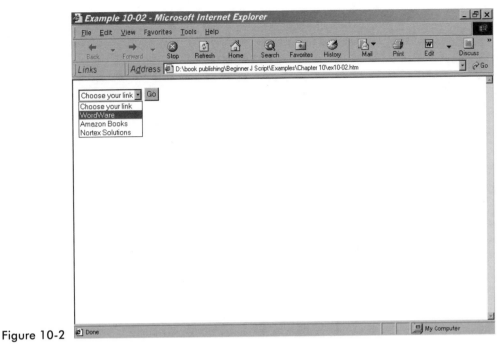

Figure 10-2

Let's take a look at the code and see what is happening. The actual script itself is amazingly simple. It is a single line of code:

```
window.location=document.dropmenu.website.options[document.dropmenu.website.
            selectedIndex].value
```

It uses the window object's location property to simply move the web page to the URL specified in the menu. This is pretty straightforward and easy to follow. The way we actually create the menu is using HTML form elements. In this case we use the select element that creates a drop-down menu. When the user has selected the web page they wish to go to, they click on the Go button and from its onClick event we call our JavaScript. This particular menu is very easy to implement, as you can see.

## Pull-Down Menus

The next type of menu we will discuss is a pull-down menu. This menu works like many applications in Microsoft Windows. With this menu example only the top-level menu title appears on the screen. When your mouse moves over that menu title, the rest of the menu drops down into view. This is a very interesting effect. Let's look at an example.

**Example 10-3**

```
<HTML>
<HEAD>
<TITLE>Example 10-03</TITLE>
<SCRIPT LANGUAGE="JavaScript">
    var browser
    if (document.getElementById)
    {
        browser = true
    }
    else
    {
        browser =  false
    }
    function toggleMenu(currElem,nextPos)
    {
        menuObj = (browser ) ? document.getElementById(currElem).style :
                     eval("document." + currElem)
        if (toggleMenu.arguments.length == 1)
        {
            nextPos = (parseInt(menuObj.top) == -5) ? -90 : -5
        }
        menuObj.top = (browser ) ? nextPos + "px" : nextPos
    }

</SCRIPT>

<STYLE TYPE="TEXT/CSS">
    .menu {position:absolute; font:12px arial, helvetica, sans-serif;
            background-color:tan; layer-background-color:tan; top:-90px}
    #fileMenu {left:10px; width:70px}
    #searchMenu {left:85px; width:100px}
    A {text-decoration:none; color:blue}
    A:hover {background-color:blue; color:red}

</STYLE>
</HEAD>
<BODY BGCOLOR="white">
<DIV ID="fileMenu" CLASS="menu" onMouseover="toggleMenu('fileMenu',-5)"
onMouseout="toggleMenu('fileMenu',-90)"><BR>
    <A HREF="javascript:window.open()">Open</A><BR>
    <A HREF="javascript:history.back()">Back</A><BR>
    <A HREF="javascript:history.forward()">Forward</A><BR>
    <A HREF="javascript:window.close()">Close</A><HR>
    <A HREF="javascript:changemenu('fileMenu')">File</A>
</DIV>
```

```
</BODY>
</HTML>
```

If you enter everything properly and then open up this web page in your browser, you should see something like the following figures.

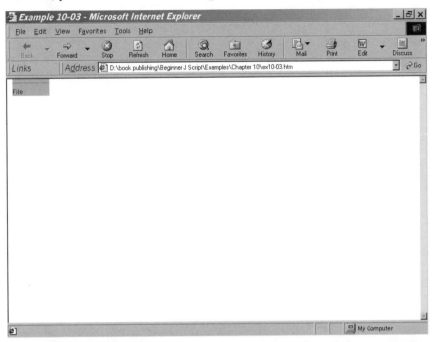

Figure 10-3

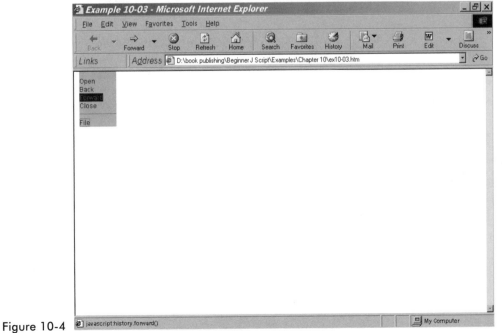

Figure 10-4

Now let's look at this example in more detail to ensure that you have a firm understanding of exactly what is occurring here.

The first part of the JavaScript code may seem a bit strange:

```
var browser
if (document.getElementById)
{
    browser = true
}
else
{
    browser =  false
}
```

What we are doing here is seeing if this browser will support the script we are writing. Since we use the document's element object, we see if this browser will support that, by simply calling the getElementById function. If this works, then the browser will support our script. You will notice that in many scripts in this book, the first step is to make sure the browser will support the script. This is simply a good practice to get into, to keep visitors to your web site from getting error messages.

The menu does most of its action in the toggleMenu function, so let's take a close look at that.

```
function toggleMenu(currElem,nextPos)
{
    menuObj = (browser ) ? document.getElementById(currElem).style :
                eval("document." + currElem)
    if (toggleMenu.arguments.length == 1)
    {
        nextPos = (parseInt(menuObj.top) == -5) ? -90 : -5
    }
    menuObj.top = (browser ) ? nextPos + "px" : nextPos
}
```

Don't let the apparent complexity scare you; this is not as tough as it looks. The real new item here is what is called a *ternary operator*. This is an operator that has three elements. Most operators you have seen so far have one or two operators (such as the unary increment operator, + +, and the binary math operators, +, –, *, /, etc.). The ternary operator has three arguments. In the form we use it here, it is essentially a condensed if-then statement. We will look closely at the second ternary operator in this script segment since it is shorter.

```
menuObj.top = (browser ) ? nextPos + "px" : nextPos
```

What is happening here is we are saying that if the browser object is valid, then menuObj.top should be set equal to nextPos + "px", otherwise simply set it to nextPos. You will see ternary operators used in many JavaScripts. They are also frequently used in Java, C , and C++ programming.

What this function does, with the use of two ternary operators simply to shorten if-else statements, is to set the position of the menu. That is, to cause it to expand so you can view the full menu or to collapse so that you cannot.

To create the menu we again use cascading style sheets. For our purposes it is not important to go into depth on the details of cascading style sheets. We can occasionally use them without an in-depth knowledge of them. We then simply use onMouseOver to display the menu and onMouseOut to make the menu disappear.

## Expanding Menus

Sometimes you have a lot of information to display, but displaying it all makes for a very cluttered web page. By using an expanding menu you can group information into topics, and then the user can click on a topic they are interested in and have the detailed information display for that topic. Let's look at an example:

**Example 10-4**

```
<HTML>
<HEAD>
<TITLE>Example 10-04</TITLE>
<SCRIPT LANGUAGE="JAVASCRIPT">
function toggleMenu(currMenu)
{
    if (document.getElementById)
    {
        thisMenu = document.getElementById(currMenu).style
            if (thisMenu.display == "block")
            {
                thisMenu.display = "none"
            }
            else
            {
                thisMenu.display = "block"
            }
                return false
```

**10**

Chapter

```
                    }
                    else
                    {
                            return true
                    }
        }
</SCRIPT>
<STYLE TYPE="TEXT/CSS">
    .menu  {display:none; margin-left:20px}
</STYLE>
</HEAD>
<BODY BGCOLOR="WHITE">
<H3>
<A HREF="example10-04.htm" onClick="return toggleMenu('menu1')">Internet
Books from WordWare</A>
</H3>
<SPAN CLASS="menu" ID="menu1">
     Learn ASP in Three Days by Jose Ramalho<BR>
     Search Engine Positioning by Fredrick Marckini<BR>
     Learn ActiveX Scripting with MSIE by Nathan Wallace<BR>
</SPAN>
<H3>
<A HREF="example10-04.htm" onClick="return toggleMenu('menu2')">Game Design
books from WordWare</A>
</H3>
<SPAN CLASS="menu" ID="menu2">
Introduction to Computer Game Programming with Direct X  8.0 by Ian Parberry<BR>
Designing Arcade Computer Game Graphics by Ari Feldman<BR>
Real-Time Strategy Game Programming using Direct X by Mickey Kawick
</SPAN>
<H3>
<A HREF="example10-04.htm" onClick="return toggleMenu('menu3')">Database
Applications from WordWare</A>
</H3>
<SPAN CLASS="menu" ID="menu3">
     Learn Microsoft SQL Server 7.0 by Jose Ramalho<BR>
     Learn Oracle 8i by Jose Ramalho
</SPAN>
</BODY>
</HTML>
```

Again we have a script that is not nearly as complicated as it looks at first glance. Let's look this script over and see what is happening.

The first thing we do is use the getElementByID function of the document object to see if this script is even supported by the browser being used. As I previously stated, it is good to get into the habit of checking to see if the browser will support your script before attempting to execute the script. Once we have confirmed that the script can be supported, we simply change the menu style from its current position. If it is currently at "none," then we display the block-style menu. If it is currently at "block" then we change it to none. What this does is cause the menu to display the first time you click, and then to disappear the second time you click.

Once again we use some cascading style sheet techniques to actually display the menu. However the call to our JavaScript function is done from a link. Since we don't actually want this link to go anywhere but to our script, I set <A HREF> to the page we are currently on.

Now if you typed in this example properly, you should be able to open it in your browser and see something like the images shown here:

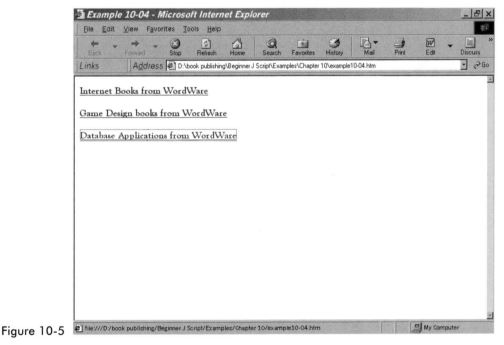

Figure 10-5

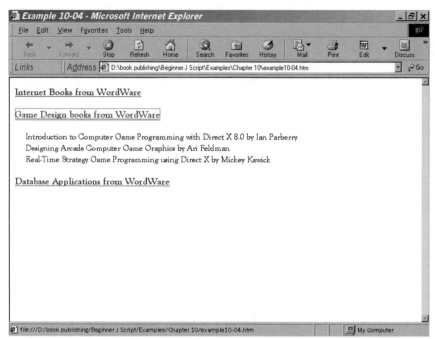

Figure 10-6

I think you will find that this particular type of menu is well suited for tasks such as displaying inventories. It allows you to initially display only categories and then the visitor to your web site can expand any category that he or she finds particularly interesting.

## Antique Bookstore Project

As with all of the chapters in this book, we will now take the techniques we have covered and incorporate them into our ongoing antique bookstore project. If you choose to work through these project exercises at the end of each chapter, then by the time you finish the book you will have built an entire web site with many exciting features.

We are going to add a complete inventory page that uses the same menu style we implemented in Example 10-4.

```
<HTML>
<HEAD>
<TITLE>Complete Inventory</TITLE>
<SCRIPT LANGUAGE="JAVASCRIPT">

function toggleMenu(currMenu)
```

```
    {
        if (document.getElementById)
        {
            thisMenu = document.getElementById(currMenu).style
                if (thisMenu.display == "block")
                {
                    thisMenu.display = "none"
                }
                else
                {
                    thisMenu.display = "block"
                }
                return false
        }
        else
        {
            return true
        }
    }

</SCRIPT>
<STYLE TYPE="TEXT/CSS">
    .menu   {display:none; margin-left:20px}
</STYLE>
</HEAD>
<BODY BGCOLOR="WHITE">


<H3>
<A HREF="completeinventory.htm"onClick="return toggleMenu('menu1')">Books
from the 1800's</A>
</H3>
<SPAN CLASS="menu" ID="menu1">
     1st Edition Charles Dickens' "Tale of Two Cities"<BR>
     1st Edition Edgar Allen Poe's "The Tell-Tale Heart"<BR>
     Signed Copy of Edgar Allen Poe's "The Cask of Amontillado"<BR>

</SPAN>
<H3>
<A HREF="completeinventory.htm" onClick="return toggleMenu('menu2')">Books
from the 1700's</A>
</H3>
<SPAN CLASS="menu" ID="menu2">
     Ben Franklin's memoirs<BR>
     "How to Start a Revolution"<BR>
     "Political Theory" by Thomas Paine<BR>
</SPAN>
```

10

Chapter

```
<H3>
<A HREF="completeinventory.htm" onClick="return toggleMenu('menu3')">Books
for under $25</A>
</H3>
<SPAN CLASS="menu" ID="menu3">
     A cowboy's diary (circa 1850's)<BR>
     4th edition Charles Dickens' "A Tale of Two Cities"<BR>
     3rd Edition Jules Verne's "20,000 Leagues Under the Sea"<BR>
</SPAN>

<H3>
<A HREF="completeinventory.htm" onClick="return toggleMenu('menu4')">Our
finest items</A>
</H3>
<SPAN CLASS="menu" ID="menu4">
     Signed copy of Shakespeare's "Hamlet"<BR>
     Gutenberg's diary<BR>
     Signed first edition Longfellow<BR>
     1570 Hebrew Bible<BR>
</SPAN>
</BODY>
</HTML>
```

## Summary

This chapter introduced you to the process of adding menus to your web pages. It gave you examples of four very different types of menus. The goal was to show you how to integrate JavaScript with other web design technologies such as HTML forms and cascading style sheets to create dynamic menus for your web site. You will find that, if you use menus on your web sites, navigation is much easier for your web sites visitors, thus increasing their satisfaction with your web page.

# Chapter 11

# Working with Forms

Throughout the past several chapters of this book you have worked with various elements of HTML forms. I have included these elements without much explanation. This chapter is devoted to explaining exactly how HTML forms function.

Essentially, HTML standards allow you to create a variety of form elements that make user input much easier. So far in this book you have already seen the text field and the button used. In this chapter we will be examining the concepts involved. We will also be looking at other form elements you can use in HTML. It is a very common technique to call your JavaScript functions from an HTML form event.

## Form Basics

Since forms are a part of HTML they are defined by tags, like everything else in HTML. The basic tag to define that you are going to use form elements is the <FORM> tag.

```
<FORM>
</FORM>
```

All of the form elements you wish to use must go between these two tags. Each form element you might wish to use is defined in a very similar way. You define the element type (button, text field, etc.), its name (what to refer to it as in your code), and its initial value. In some cases you also define other properties such as size. For example, if you wish to place a text field on your HTML document so your users can enter data it works like this:

**Example 11-1**

```
<HTML>
<HEAD>
```

```
        <TITLE>Example 11-01</TITLE>
</HEAD>
<BODY>
<FORM>
    <INPUT TYPE=text NAME="txttest" VALUE="Enter Text Here">
<FORM>
</BODY>
</HTML>
```

If you enter all the code correctly, you should be able to view the page in your browser and see something similar to this:

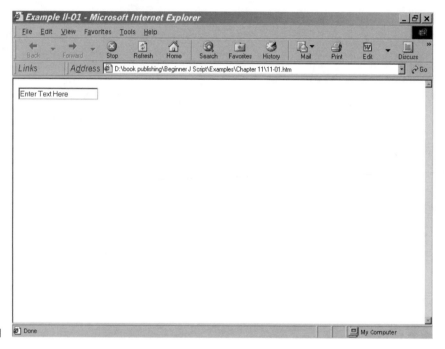

Figure 11-1

As you can see in this example, inside the <FORM> and </FORM> tags we define the form elements we wish to display. The first thing we define is what type of form element it will be. In this example it is a text field. We then give it a name. We can use that name later in either HTML or in our JavaScript to refer to that form element. Finally, we put an initial value in the text field; this is optional. As you can see, creating form elements is rather simple.

# Text Fields and Buttons

Possibly the two most commonly used form elements are the text field (which we saw in the previous example) and the button. The button is an excellent form element to call your JavaScripts from. Let's look at an example that does just that.

**Example 11-2**

```
<HTML>
<HEAD>
    <TITLE>Example 11-02</TITLE>
    <SCRIPT LANGUAGE = "JavaScript">
        alert(txttest.value)
    </SCRIPT>
</HEAD>
<BODY>
<CENTER>
    <INPUT TYPE=text NAME="txttest" VALUE="Enter Text Here"><BR>
    <INPUT TYPE=button NAME="Submit" VALUE="Submit" onclick="test()">
</CENTER>
</BODY>
</HTML>
```

This example shows a minor but important twist on the usage of form elements. Here we have a button, and when it is clicked (onClick event) we call a JavaScript function. This function, in turn, references the value in the HTML form's text field. If you enter all the code properly you will be able to see something very similar to the following figure:

**11**

Chapter

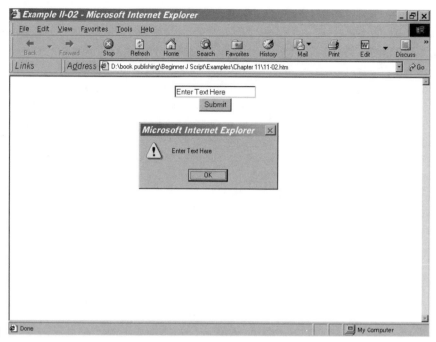

Figure 11-2

Using buttons to trigger JavaScript functions is both quite common and very useful. This technique allows you to call functions in response to user activity. In our example, the JavaScript we call is quite simple, but it illustrates the point quite well.

## Options

An option in HTML is the same thing as a combo box in Visual Basic. It is a drop-down box that displays a list of choices from which the user can select. This can be quite useful if you wish the user to select from multiple items but do not wish to clutter your screen. Consider the following example:

### Example 11-3

```
<HTML>
<HEAD>
    <TITLE> Example 11-03</TITLE>
<SCRIPT>
function moveon()
{
    window.location=document.dropdown.selection.options[document.
        dropdown.selection.selectedIndex].value
}
```

```
</SCRIPT>
<BODY BGCOLOR = "White">
<FORM NAME="dropdown">
    <SELECT NAME="selection"
    <OPTION VALUE=""><B>Select an Option</B>
    <OPTION VALUE="this.html">this one
    <OPTION VALUE="next.html">next one
    <OPTION VALUE="after.html">one after
    </SELECT>
    <INPUT TYPE=button NAME="Submit" VALUE="Submit" onclick="moveon()">
</FORM>
</BODY>
</HTML>
```

This example simply allows the user to select which web page they would like
to navigate to. Once they have selected the page, they press the Submit button
and are taken to that page. The script is actually only one line. It simply uses
the window.location property to move to whatever web page the user selected.
If you enter the code properly, you should be able to see something like this:

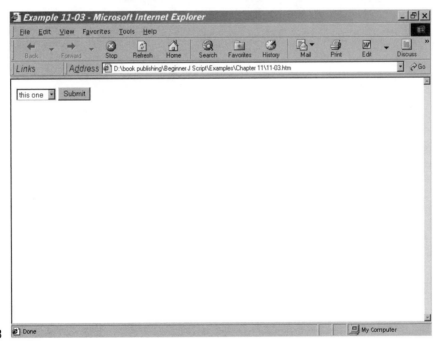

Figure 11-3

## Radio Buttons

Radio buttons are the small circles that you click to select a particular option. You have seen these before in web pages and on desktop applications. Radio buttons present a series of choices to the user, of which the user may select only one. Look at this example:

**Example 11-4**

```
<HTML>
<HEAD>
     <TITLE>Example 11-04</TITLE>
<SCRIPT LANGUAGE="JavaScript">
</SCRIPT>
</HEAD>
<BODY>
<FORM>
    <INPUT TYPE="radio" NAME="radiobutton" onClick="radio_selection='A'">Add
    <INPUT TYPE="radio" NAME="radiobutton" onClick="radio_selection='D'">Delete
    <INPUT TYPE="radio" NAME="radiobutton" onClick="radio_selection='U'">Update
</FORM>
</HTML>
```

As you can see, we simply use INPUT TYPE="radio" to indicate that this is going to be an input type, and the input will be done via a radio button. We then give the radio buttons a name. Notice they all have the same name. Since the user can only select one button, we are simply interested in setting the value based on one button.

If you enter the code exactly as shown in the example, you will then be able to see the following screen:

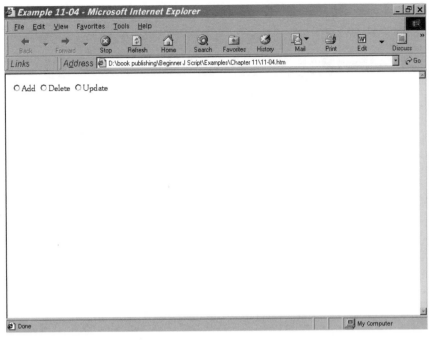

Figure 11-4

## Check Boxes

Radio buttons present several choices but only allow you to select one. This is very useful in many cases, such as if you are asking the user's marital status: married, single, or divorced. They can only be one at any given time. However, with other types of information a person might be able to select more than one choice. For example, if you ask a person to indicate which sports they watch on TV (football, basketball, baseball, golf), they may want to choose more than one. For this type of data, you should use a check box. A check box is similar to an option box, but the person can select multiple options. The following example illustrates this.

**Example 11-5**

```
<HTML>
<HEAD>
    <TITLE>Example 11-05</TITLE>
<SCRIPT LANGUAGE="JavaScript">
var allchecked = "false"
function check(field)
{
    if (allchecked  == "false")
    {
```

11

Chapter

```
                    for (i = 0; i < field.length; i++)
                    {
                         field[i].checked = true;
                    }
               allchecked  = "true"
               return "Uncheck All"
          }
          else
          {
                    for (i = 0; i < field.length; i++)
                    {
                         field[i].checked = false
                    }
          allchecked  = "false"
          return "Check All"
          }
    }

</SCRIPT>
</HEAD>
<BODY BGCOLOR = White>
<FORM NAME =myform>
<b>JavaScript Websites you like!</b><br>
<INPUT TYPE=checkbox name=list value="1">JavaScript Source<BR>
<INPUT TYPE=checkbox name=list value="2">JavaScript.Com<BR>
<INPUT TYPE=checkbox name=list value="3">JavaScript World<BR>
<INPUT TYPE=checkbox name=list value="4">HTML Goodies <BR>
<BR>
<INPUT TYPE=button VALUE="Check All" onClick="this.value=check(this.form.list)">
</FORM>
</HTML>
```

In this example we use the <FORM> tag to indicate that form elements are going to be used. We then use INPUT TYPE=checkbox. This lets the browser know it should display a check box. If you enter all the code properly, you should see something like the following screen.

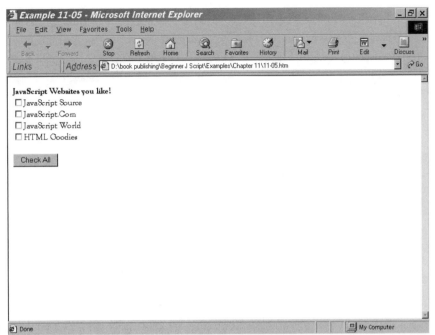

Figure 11-5

The check box can be very useful in allowing the user to select multiple options.

## Event Handlers in Form Elements

There are a variety of event handlers that allow you to invoke specific JavaScript code when the user performs a given action. We will examine a few of the most common here.

### onSubmit

The onSubmit event handler is an attribute of the <FORM> tag. It is called when a form is submitted. A form can be submitted in several ways; the Submit button is only one of many. The submit event can occur immediately upon clicking a submit button, pressing Enter, or several other methods. JavaScript triggers this event prior to sending the data to the server. The event handler's script is executed before the form's data is actually submitted to the server for further processing.

11

Chapter

The onSubmit event handler is commonly used to validate the content of a form's element. Client-side form validation is gaining popularity because the user receives an immediate response regarding invalid entries. For example, if you have a form with a text box in which the user is asked to type his or her e-mail address, you can use a simple JavaScript script that will make sure (upon submission) the user's entry is a string containing an "at" sign (@), which, of course, all valid e-mail address will have.

You can use the onSubmit event handler not just to validate the form's elements but also to cancel its submission altogether. The form's submission is aborted when the event handler returns a false value, as in the following example:

```
<FORM NAME="form1" onSubmit="return false">
```

Of course, this example is not very useful because it disables the form submission unconditionally. However, it does illustrate the point in question. Usually, a function validates the form and returns a true or false value accordingly. You can use the following code to cancel or proceed with the form submission, depending on the value returned by the function:

```
<FORM NAME="form1" onSubmit="return checkData()">
```

The following example illustrates these concepts with a form containing a text area box and a Submit button which e-mails you the contents of the text area after prompting the user for confirmation:

**Example 11-6**

```
<SCRIPT LANGUAGE="JavaScript">
function continue()
{
    return confirm("Click OK to mail this information")
}

</SCRIPT>
<FORM ACTION="mailto:chuckeasttom@yahoo.com" METHOD="post" ENCTYPE=
            "text/plain" onSubmit="return continue()">
    <INPUT TYPE =textfield NAME="txttest" Value = "Put Message Here"><BR>
    <INPUT TYPE=button VALUE="Send Mail">
</FORM>
```

If you enter all the code correctly, you should be able to use your browser and see the following image:

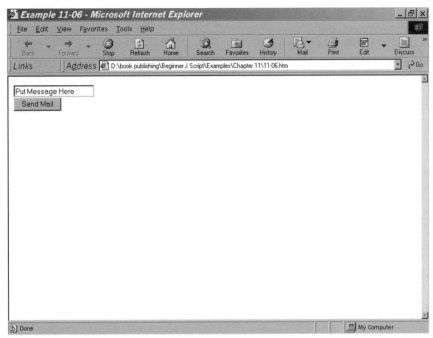

Figure 11-6

Some of the parameters used here you have seen before, but ENCTYPE may be new to you. In order to receive the form's content as a plain, unscrambled e-mail, you need to assign a text/plain value to the ENCTYPE attribute.

## onReset

Another event handler of the <FORM> tag is onReset. A reset event usually occurs when the user clicks a Reset button. The onReset event handler behaves very much like the onSubmit event handler.

The following example asks the user to confirm the resetting process before executing it:

**Example 11-7**

```
<HTML>
<HEAD>
    <TITLE>Example 11-07</TITLE>
</HEAD>
<BODY BGCOLOR = White>
<FORM ACTION="mailto:chuckeasttom@yahoo.com" METHOD="post" ENCTYPE="text/plain"
onReset="return confirm('Click OK to reset form to default status')">
<TEXTAREA NAME="input" COLS=40 ROWS=10></TEXTAREA><BR>
<INPUT TYPE="reset" VALUE="reset it!">
```

11

Chapter

```
    </FORM>
    </BODY>
    </HTML>
```

In this example, if you press the Reset button, you are prompted to confirm the action. Then all the text is reset to its default value, which happens to be blank. If you enter all the code correctly, you should be able to use your browser and see the following image:

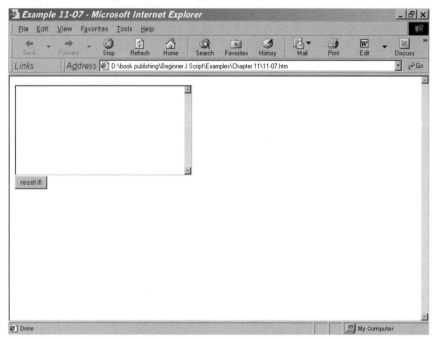

Figure 11-7

## Synopsis of Form Elements

The following table summarizes the major form elements available to you in HTML.

| HTML Element | Value of Type Attribute |
| --- | --- |
| INPUT TYPE="button" | "button" |
| INPUT TYPE="checkbox" | "checkbox" |
| INPUT TYPE="file" | "file" |
| INPUT TYPE="hidden" | "hidden" |
| INPUT TYPE="password" | "password" |
| INPUT TYPE="radio" | "radio" |
| INPUT TYPE="reset" | "reset" |
| INPUT TYPE="submit" | "submit" |

| HTML Element | Value of Type Attribute |
|---|---|
| INPUT TYPE="text" | "text" |
| SELECT | "select-one" |

## Antique Bookstore Project

This chapter is one of the rare ones where we do not add a new item to our antique bookstore project. This is because we have already used form elements in previous chapters. This chapter's goal was simply to clarify form issues.

## Summary

Throughout this book we have used form elements. Prior to this chapter you have simply typed them in and may not have realized exactly what you were doing. After studying this chapter you should have a good understanding of how HTML forms work.

**11**

Chapter

# Chapter 12

# Strings in JavaScript

Strings have many uses in your scripts. Strings hold text data, such as names, addresses, etc. You can store string values in a standard variable. However, if you create a string object to store your string data, you then can use the various string object methods to manipulate that string. Essentially, strings are simply an array of individual characters. The indexing of strings, like that of arrays, is zero-based. The index of the first character of a string is 0, the index of the second one is 1, that of the third one is 2, and so on.

## Creating Strings

String is a built-in object. This means that it is handled a bit differently than other variables. It is created like an object variable, rather than like a simple variable. Here is an example:

```
var lastname = new String("Smith")
```

The general syntax is:

```
Var name = new String(string)
```

*name* is the name of the string object you are creating. You can give it any name you wish, but I recommend a name that reflects the type of data it will hold. *string* is any literal string, as in the example.

### String Length

The String object combines many useful methods and one property, length. This property reflects the length of its calling object. Here is an example:

**Example 12-1**

```
<HTML>
<HEAD>
```

```
                    <TITLE>Example 12-01</TITLE>
                    <SCRIPT LANGUAGE = "JavaScript">
                        function test()
                        {
                            var mystr =txttest.value
                            alert(mystr.length)


                        }
                    </SCRIPT>
            </HEAD>
            <BODY>
            <CENTER>
                <INPUT TYPE=text NAME="txttest" VALUE="Enter Text Here"><BR>
                <INPUT TYPE=button NAME="Submit" VALUE="Submit" onclick="test()">
            </CENTER>
            </BODY>
            </HTML>
```

If you enter the example properly, you can use your browser to view it and you should see the following:

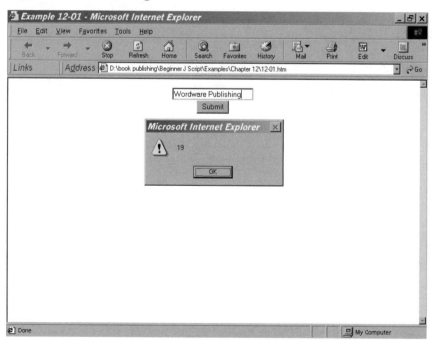

Figure 12-1

# String Methods

As mentioned, the String object has many useful methods, one of which is the toUpperCase() method. This changes all the text in the string to uppercase. There are many practical applications for this method.

### charAt()

The charAt() method returns the character whose index is equal to the argument of the method. The characters of a string are indexed from 0 to length–1. The general syntax is:

```
mystring.charAt(index)
```

Here is an example:

**Example 12-2**

```
<HTML>
<HEAD>
    <TITLE>Example 12-02</TITLE>
    <SCRIPT LANGUAGE = "JavaScript">
        function test()
        {
            var mystr =txttest.value
            alert(mystr.charAt(1))

        }
    </SCRIPT>
</HEAD>

<BODY>
<CENTER>
    <INPUT TYPE=text NAME="txttest" VALUE="Enter Text Here"><BR>
    <INPUT TYPE=button NAME="Submit" VALUE="Submit" onclick="test()">
</CENTER>
</BODY>
</HTML>
```

If you entered the code properly, and then entered some text in the box you should see something similar to the following figure:

**12**

Chapter

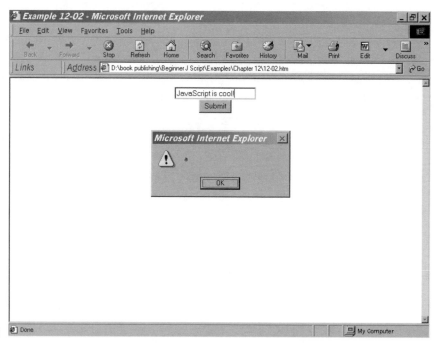

Figure 12-2

The following script segment prints the character "o," because it is the second character (index 1) in the string. You can also call this method with a literal text as in the following example:

```
document.write("wordware".charAt(1))
```

You can print the characters of a string via a simple loop:

```
var mystring = "Wordware Publishing"
for (var i = 0; i < mystring.length; ++i)
{
    document.write(mystring.charAt(i))
}
```

At first, a string literal is assigned to the variable mystring. The loop then iterates length times. It starts at 0, and ends at mystring.length–1.

### indexOf()

This method returns the index of the first occurrence of the specified substring in the calling string object, starting the search at the beginning of the string. An example will surely clear things up:

```
var mystring = "wordware"
document.write(str.indexOf("wo"))
```

This script's output is the number 0. The first occurrence of the substring "wo" in the calling string object is at the second character whose index is 0. The search for the specified substring starts at index 0, the beginning of the string.

## lastIndexOf()

This method is identical to the indexOf method, except that it returns the index of the last occurrence of the specified value, rather than the first occurrence. Its syntax is, obviously, the same:

```
stringName.lastIndexOf(searchValue, [fromIndex])
```

The following script prints the number 3:

```
var mystring = "a/b/c"
document.write(str.lastIndexOf("/"))
```

## substring()

Strings are constructed of characters. The substring() method returns a set of characters within its calling String object. Its general syntax is:

```
stringName.substring(indexA, indexB)
```

*stringName* is any string. *indexA* and *indexB* are both integers between 0 and *stringName*.length – 1. *indexA* is the index of the first character in the substring, whereas *indexB* is the index of the last character in the substring plus 1. Consider the following example:

### Example 12-3

```
<HTML>
<HEAD>
    <TITLE>Example 12-03</TITLE>
    <SCRIPT LANGUAGE = "JavaScript">
        function test()
        {
            var begin = txtbegin.value
            var end = txtend.value
            var mystring =txttest.value
            var seg = mystring.substring(begin,end)
            alert(seg)

        }
    </SCRIPT>
```

**12**

Chapter

```
    </HEAD>

    <BODY>
    <CENTER>
        <INPUT TYPE=text NAME="txttest" VALUE="Enter Text Here"><BR>
        <INPUT TYPE=text NAME="txtbegin" VALUE="0">
        <INPUT TYPE=text NAME="txtend" VALUE="5"><BR>
        <INPUT TYPE=button NAME="Submit" VALUE="Submit" onclick="test()">
    </CENTER>
    </BODY>
    </HTML>
```

If you entered everything properly, you should see something like the following in your browser:

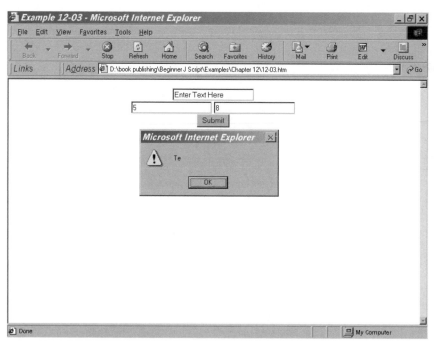

Figure 12-3

Notice that the length of the substring is *indexA – indexB*.

# Number-to-String Conversion

Occasionally, you need to convert a number to a string. For example, if you want to compute the number of digits in a number, you can convert it to a string and use the length property, which applies to strings only. In this section we shall take a look at a few ways to convert a number to a string.

### Empty String Concatenation

The easiest way to convert a number to a string is by concatenating an empty string to the number. Here is an example:

```
var num = 2001
num = num + ""
```

You can also convert the number to a string and assign the numeric string to another variable, or, even better, do both operations in one statement:

```
var num = 2001
var numericString = num + ""
```

## Antique Bookstore Project

Most of the chapters in this book end by adding something to our ongoing antique bookstore project. However, this chapter is more about some useful techniques for string manipulation and is not easily suited to our ongoing project. For this reason, this chapter will not be adding to our project. However, don't worry, the next chapter will add plenty!

## Summary

While you can store string data in a standard variable, I hope you have seen that the String object can be quite useful. You will find many practical situations where you will need to know a string's length or other properties. You may also need to periodically manipulate the contents of a string. With JavaScript's String object you can do that.

**12**

Chapter

# Chapter 13

# Math in JavaScript

We have been able to do a lot of interesting things without using any math. However, at some point you will probably need to use math in your JavaScript. This is especially true for business web sites.

Math in JavaScript is basically divided into two areas:

- Mathematical operators
- The built-in Math object

## Mathematical Operators

You are probably familiar with most math operators. They were introduced to you in Chapter 2. But just in case you need a bit of a refresher, the following table should help you.

| Operator | Symbol | Explanation | Example |
|---|---|---|---|
| Addition | + | Adds the numbers on either side together | Var mynum<br>Mynum = mynum + 1 |
| Subtraction | – | Subtracts the number on the right from the number on the left | Var mynum = mynum – 1 |
| Multiplication | * | Multiplies the numbers on either side together | Var mynum = mynum * 5 |
| Division | / | Divides the number on the left side by the number on the right side | Var mynumMynum = mynum /4 |
| Modulus | % | Provides you with the remainder of a division operation | Var answerAnswer = 9%4(answer will be 1) |
| Increment | ++ | Increments the number by one | Var mynumMynum++ |
| Decrement | – – | Decreases the number by one | Var mynumMynum– – |

Here is a piece of code that uses these operators in conjunction with form elements to create a simple calculator.

**Example 13-1**

```
<HTML>
<HEAD>
    <TITLE>Example 13-01</TITLE>
</HEAD>
<BODY>
<CENTER>
<FORM NAME="calculator">
<TABLE BORDER=1 BGCOLOR = green>
    <TR>
        <TD>
            <INPUT TYPE="text"    NAME="Input" Size="16">
          <BR>
        <TR>
        <TD>
            <INPUT TYPE="button" NAME="one"    VALUE="  1   "
                OnClick="calculator.Input.value += '1'">
            <INPUT TYPE="button" NAME="two"    VALUE="  2   "
                OnCLick="calculator.Input.value += '2'">
            <INPUT TYPE="button" NAME="three" VALUE="  3   "
                OnClick="calculator.Input.value += '3'">
            <INPUT TYPE="button" NAME="plus"  VALUE="  +   "
                OnClick="calculator.Input.value += ' + '">
        <TR>
        <TD>
            <INPUT TYPE="button" NAME="four"   VALUE="  4   "
                OnClick="calculator.Input.value += '4'">
            <INPUT TYPE="button" NAME="five"  VALUE="  5   "
                OnCLick="calculator.Input.value += '5'">
            <INPUT TYPE="button" NAME="six"    VALUE="  6   "
                OnClick="calculator.Input.value += '6'">
            <INPUT TYPE="button" NAME="minus" VALUE="  -   "
                OnClick="calculator.Input.value += ' - '">
        <TR>
        <TD>
            <INPUT TYPE="button" NAME="seven" VALUE="  7   "
                OnClick="calculator.Input.value += '7'">
            <INPUT TYPE="button" NAME="eight" VALUE="  8   "
                OnClick="calculator.Input.value += '8'">
            <INPUT TYPE="button" NAME="nine"  VALUE="  9   "
                OnClick="calculator.Input.value += '9'">
            <INPUT TYPE="button" NAME="times" VALUE="  x   "
                OnClick="calculator.Input.value += ' * '">
```

```
      <TR>
         <TD>
            <INPUT TYPE="button" NAME="clear" VALUE="  c  "
               OnClick="calculator.Input.value = ''">
            <INPUT TYPE="button" NAME="zero"  VALUE="  0  "
               OnClick="calculator.Input.value += '0'">
            <INPUT TYPE="button" NAME="DoIt"  VALUE="  =  "
               OnClick="calculator.Input.value =
               eval(calculator.Input.value)">
            <INPUT TYPE="button" NAME="div"   VALUE="  /  "
               OnClick="calculator.Input.value += ' / '">
   <BR>

   </TABLE>
   </FORM>
   </CENTER>
   </BODY>
   </HTML>
```

# The Math Object

In the previous chapter you were introduced to the JavaScript String object. In this chapter I will introduce you to the JavaScript Math object. This object has a variety of mathematical functions that you may find quite useful in your scripts.

To access elements of the Math object, you do not need to create an instance of the Math object. For example, the PI constant is a property of the Math object, and can be accessed via the following syntax:

```
var pi = Math.PI
```

Notice you did not have to establish a variable for the Math object itself.

## Constants

There are a number of math constants built into the Math object. These constants are simply mathematical constants that are frequently used. Some of them, at least, should be familiar to you. If any are unfamiliar, then simply skip them. If you don't know what a particular mathematical constant is, chances are you won't need to use it in your scripts.

### E

A very important constant in mathematics is Euler's constant. Its approximate value is 2.718281828459045. It is rounded off to 15 digits after the decimal point.

In JavaScript you refer to it via a capital E; that is, Math.E. (In mathematics it is usually referred to with a lowercase "e.")

### LN2

Another constant featured as a property of the Math object is the natural logarithm of 2. Its approximate value is 0.6931471805599453.

JavaScript refers to this number as LN2. Because it is a property of the Math object, you should specify them together, as in Math.LN2.

You can use the pow method to assure that the preceding equation is true:

```
document.write(Math.pow(Math.E, Math.LN2))
```

Because both Euler's constant and the natural logarithm of 2 are approximate, the output of this statement is also an approximate:

```
1.9999999999999998
```

### LN10

The natural logarithm of 10 is also featured as a property of the static Math object. Its value, as stored in its corresponding property, is 2.302585092994046.

In JavaScript this value is referred to as Math.LN10.

Here is a JavaScript statement to define the natural logarithm of 10:

```
document.write(Math.pow(Math.E, Math.LN10))
```

Since both Euler's constant and the natural logarithm of 10 are approximate, the output of this statement is also approximate:

```
10.000000000000002
```

### LOG2E

Another important constant in the math arena is the base-2 logarithm of Euler's constant. Its approximate value is 1.4426950408889634. In math that is:

$$2^{LOG2E} = e$$

As you can see, you refer to this constant in JavaScript as Math.LOG2E. Here is a simple statement to confirm the value:

```
document.write(Math.pow(2, Math.LOG2E) — Math.E)
```

This time the output is apparently exact:

```
0
```

### LOG10E

The base-10 logarithm is also widely used in complex mathematical calculations. Its value in JavaScript is approximately 0.4342944819032518.

As you can see, the equation is built according to one of the basic logarithm rules. In JavaScript, log base-10 of Euler's constant is a property of the Math object: Math.LOG10E.

Here is a simple script for confirmation:

```
document.write(Math.pow(10, Math.LOG10E) — Math.E)
```

Once again, the output is exact:

```
0
```

### PI

Probably the most known value among all constants featured by JavaScript is PI. PI is used in many equations involving calculations with circles. Its approximate value is 3.14.

### SQRT2

The square root of 2 is also a well-known constant. Its approximate value is 1.4142135623730951. You refer to it as Math.SQRT2. You can use the following statement to ensure the value:

```
document.write(Math.pow(Math.SQRT2, 2))
```

As you could expect, the result is not an exact one:

```
2.0000000000000004
```

## Math Methods

Constants are interesting, but for most business applications you won't need to use any of these mathematical constants. On the other hand, the methods of the Math object will probably be very useful to you.

The methods of the Math object can be divided into two categories:

- Arithmetic methods
- Trigonometric methods

## Arithmetic Methods

Let's start by examining the arithmetic methods since they are used more frequently.

### abs()

You can calculate the absolute value of any number by using this method. The absolute value of a number is its distance from zero.

For example, the absolute value of –5 is 5. The absolute value of 5 is also 5. In JavaScript you can calculate the absolute value of a number via the method Math.abs(). This method returns the absolute value of its argument.

### ceil()

The Math.ceil() method accepts a single numeric argument and returns the next integer greater than or equal to the argument (rounding up). Therefore, the returned value is never less than the argument. Here are a few examples:

```
Math.ceil(16) == 16
Math.ceil(16.01) == 17
Math.ceil(-15.01) == -15
```

Now if you are wondering when you would ever use this function, don't worry, I have a practical example for you. Let's say you need to fit a certain number of people into a conference room where each table can only seat four people. You can use the Math.ceil() method along with a function to calculate the minimum number of tables:

```
function getNumLots(numpeople)
{
    return Math.ceil(numpeople / 4)
}
```

Since you cannot use a part of a table, this method helps us find out how many tables we need.

### floor()

The Math.floor() method is virtually identical to the ceiling method except that it returns the greatest integer less than or equal to the value passed to it. Here are a few examples:

```
Math.floor(16) == 16
Math.floor(16.01) == 16
Math.floor(-15.01) == -16
```

## log()

This method simply returns the natural logarithm of the argument passed to it.

## max(), min()

Both of these methods accept two numeric arguments. max() returns the greater of two numbers, whereas min() returns the lesser of the two. Here is a function that prints the lesser of two numbers followed by the greater:

```
function printInOrder(num1, num2)
{
    document.write(Math.min(num1, num2) + ", " + Math.max(num1, num2))
}
```

The following function call prints the string "–5, 1" to the document:

```
printInOrder(1, -5)
```

Here are a few true expressions to demonstrate the basic min() and max() methods:

```
Math.max(1, 2) == 2
Math.min(2, Math.abs(-2)) == 2
Math.min(2, -2) == -2
```

## pow()

Given two numeric arguments, this method returns the first one to the power of the second. Here are a few true expressions demonstrating the method:

```
Math.pow(10, 2) == 100
Math.pow(5,3) == 125
```

## round()

The Math.round() method rounds a number to the nearest integer. If the argument's decimal part is equal to 0.5, the number is rounded upward. Here are a few :

```
Math.round(3.7) == 4
Math.round(4.5) == 5
Math.round(16.1) == 16
Math.round(0) == 0
```

### sqrt()

This method returns the square root of the argument. For example:

```
Math.sqrt(4) == 2
Math.sqrt(0) == 0
Math.sqrt(0.25) == 0.5
```

If the argument is a negative number, the method returns zero, which happens to be the wrong answer. JavaScript is not able to return imaginary numbers (which are the square roots of negative numbers).

## Trigonometric Methods

Trigonometric methods are obviously those that deal with trigonometry. Now if you don't know anything about trigonometry, don't worry about it. You can be quite a successful JavaScript programmer without using trigonometry. All angles in JavaScript are measured by radians rather than degrees because that is the standard used in trigonometry.

### cos()

Math.cos() takes just one argument, the angle of a triangle. It returns the cosine of that value, which we know must be specified in radians. Here is an example that prints out –1.

```
document.write(Math.cos(Math.PI))
```

The other trigonometric methods—sin, asin, acos, tan, atan—all work the same way. Here is an example that computes each of the trigonometric functions for a given angle:

**Example 13-2**

```
<HTML>
<HEAD>
    <TITLE>Example 13-02</TITLE>
    <SCRIPT LANGUAGE = "JavaScript">
        function trig()
        {
            var temp
            var angle
            angle = txttest.value

            temp = Math.sin(angle)
            txtsin.value = temp

            temp = Math.cos(angle)
```

```
                    txtcos.value = temp

                    temp = Math.tan(angle)
                    txttan.value = temp

                    temp = Math.asin(angle)
                    txtasin.value = temp

                    temp = Math.acos(angle)
                    txtacos.value = temp

                    temp = Math.atan(angle)
                    txtatan.value = temp
                }
        </SCRIPT>
    </HEAD>

    <BODY>
    <TABLE BORDER = 1 BGCOLOR = GRAY >
        <TR>
            <TD>
                Angle <INPUT TYPE=text NAME="txttest" VALUE=""><BR>
                <INPUT TYPE=button NAME="Submit" VALUE="Compute"
                            onclick="trig()">
            <TD>
                <INPUT TYPE=text NAME="txtsin" VALUE=""> Sine  <BR>
                <INPUT TYPE=text NAME="txtcos" VALUE=""> Cosine<BR>
                <INPUT TYPE=text NAME="txttan" VALUE=""> Tangent<BR>
                <INPUT TYPE=text NAME="txtasin" VALUE=""> Arc sine  <BR>
                <INPUT TYPE=text NAME="txtacos" VALUE=""> Arc cosine <BR>
                <INPUT TYPE=text NAME="txtatan" VALUE="">Arc tangent<BR>
    </BODY>
    </HTML>
```

If you enter in all the code properly, you should be able to open your browser and see an image much like the following:

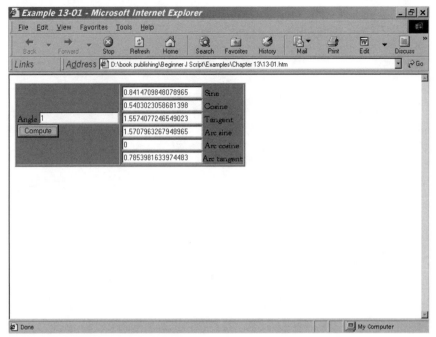

Figure 13-1

## Antique Bookstore Project

As with most of the chapters in this book we are going to use some of the techniques presented in our antique bookstore project. Obviously the trigonometry functions and many of the constants are not going to be of particular use for an antique bookstore. However, the basic math operators will be. We will add a screen that allows users to compute sales tax and shipping costs for books.

```
<HTML>
<HEAD>
    <TITLE>Computer Costs</TITLE>

<SCRIPT LANGUAGE="JAVASCRIPT" >
function total()
{
    var shipping
    var tax
    var total

    var numbooks = txtbooks.value
    var price = txtprice.value
```

```
        tax = price * .0875
        shipping = numbooks * 1.5
        total = eval(price) + eval(tax) + eval(shipping)

        txttax.value = tax
        txtship.value = shipping
        txttotal.value = total
}


</SCRIPT
</HEAD>
<BODY    background="back1.gif" >
<P>
<CENTER>
<TABLE BORDER = 1>
    <TR>
        <TD>
            Number of books ordered <INPUT TYPE=text NAME="txtbooks"
                    VALUE=""><BR>
            Total price of books ordered<INPUT TYPE = text NAME = "txtprice"
                    VALUE = ""><BR>
            <INPUT TYPE=button NAME="Submit" VALUE="Compute"
                    onclick="total()">

    <TR>
        <TD>
            <INPUT TYPE=text NAME="txttax" VALUE=""> Tax<BR>
            <INPUT TYPE=text NAME="txtship" VALUE="">Shipping Costs <BR>
            <INPUT TYPE=text NAME="txttotal" VALUE=""> Total<BR>
</TABLE>
</CENTER>
</BODY>
</HTML>
```

If you enter all the code correctly, you can use your browser to view the page and see something like the following screen.

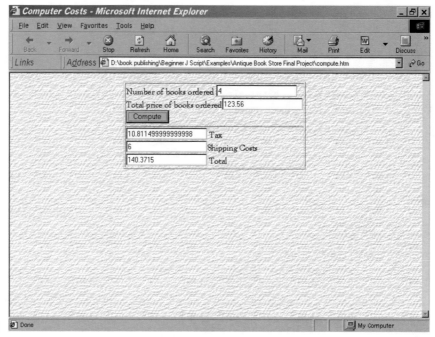

Figure 13-2

## Summary

This chapter should have given you an overview of the various math functions built into JavaScript. It is by no means a comprehensive coverage of math in JavaScript. It should, however, give you all the mathematical tools you will need to write some very powerful JavaScripts.

# Chapter 14

# Adding Plug-ins

This chapter ventures into a more advanced HTML topic, that of plug-ins. Plug-ins are essentially objects you insert into your HTML document to provide some added functionality, usually multimedia. If you have ever been to a site that required you to download some component to view the site, then you have used plug-ins.

Strictly speaking, plug-ins are not JavaScript. However, JavaScript is about creating high-quality web sites and I would be remiss in my duties if I did not provide you with this introduction here. Considering the wide range of JavaScript techniques you have already been shown, adding plug-ins will allow you to create some truly spectacular web sites.

## Putting a Plug-in into Your HTML

A *plug-in* is a piece of software that the browser calls to process data referenced in an HTML document. In order to reference such data in an HTML tag, you must use the <EMBED> tag. This tag's general format is as follows:

```
<EMBED
    SRC=source
    NAME=appletName
    HEIGHT=height
    WIDTH=width>
    [<PARAM NAME=parameterName VALUE=parameterValue>]
    [...<PARAM>]
</EMBED>
```

SRC=*source* specifies the URL containing the source content to be interpreted by the plug-in. This may be some external URL, or could simply be a part of your own web site where you store the plug-in for downloading.

NAME=*appletName* specifies the name of the embedded object in the document. This name can be just about anything. It is simply the name you will use to reference the plug-in from within your web page.

HEIGHT=*height* specifies the height of the applet in pixels within the browser window.

WIDTH=*width* specifies the width of the applet in pixels within the browser window.

<PARAM> defines a parameter for the embedded object.

NAME=*parameterName* specifies the name of the parameter.

VALUE=*parameterValue* specifies a value for the parameter (an argument).

We will refer to such <EMBED> definitions as plug-ins, although that is not entirely correct.

## Using Plug-ins in JavaScript

You can use the plug-ins in your JavaScript code by simply referencing the name you give the plug-in when you embed it. In fact, that is what that name is for. You can also embed plug-ins into an array called embeds, and then reference that element of the embeds array that has your plug-in.

```
document.embeds[0]="myVideo.avi"
```

You can also reference a plug-in object by its name. Take a look at the following HTML definition:

```
<EMBED SRC="mymovie.avi" AUTOSTART=FALSE LOOP=FALSE HEIGHT=120 WIDTH=159
NAME="mymovie">
```

Now you can reference this plug-in's properties and methods by simply calling mymovie.method() (substitute the actual method name). You can also reference it by using the embeds array. For example, if your plug-in were the first one embedded, you could reference it like this:

```
document.embeds[0]
```

Now for a little treat. In the Chapter 14 folder of the code files, I have included an ActiveX component (plug-in) that I created. This plug-in allows you to send TCP packets to any valid IP address or URL. I have a little sample code here using it:

**Example 14-1**

```
<HTML>
<HEAD>
<script language ="JavaScript">
function send()
{
    var ip
    var port
    var data
    var result

    ip =frmip.ipaddress.value
    port =frmport.port.value
    data =frmdata.data.value

    TCPClient.remoteIP =ip
    TCPClient.remotePort =port
    TCPClient.Message =data

    result =TCPClient.sendData()
    alert(result)
}
</script>


<TITLE>Example 14-01</TITLE>
</HEAD>

<BODY BGCOLOR = White>
<OBJECT ID="TCPClient"
    CLASSID="CLSID:26900070-7443-11D5-9A47-00409639327E"
    CODEBASE="TCPClientControl.CAB#version=2,0,0,0">
</OBJECT>
<TABLE BORDER = 1>
    <TR>
    <TD>
    <TABLE border=0 CellPadding = 0 CellSpacing = 0>
        <TR>
            <TD>
                <B>IP Address<B>
            <TD>
            <BR>
            <FORM name ="frmip">
                <INPUT TYPE="text" NAME ="ipaddress" VALUE="" SIZE=10>
            </FORM>
```

14

Chapter

```
        <TR>
            <TD>
                <B>Port<B>
            <TD>
            <BR>
            <FORM NAME ="frmport">
                <INPUT TYPE="text" NAME = "port" VALUE="" SIZE=10>
            </FORM>
        <TR>
            <TD>
                <B> Data to send<B>
            <TD>
            <BR>
            <FORM NAME ="frmdata">
                <INPUT TYPE="text" NAME ="data" VALUE="" SIZE=10>
            </FORM>
        <TR>
            <TD>
            <CENTER>
                <INPUT TYPE="button" VALUE="Submit" onClick="send()">
            </CENTER>
        </TABLE>
    </CENTER>
    </BODY>
    </HTML>
```

If you enter the code properly, you will be able to view something like this:

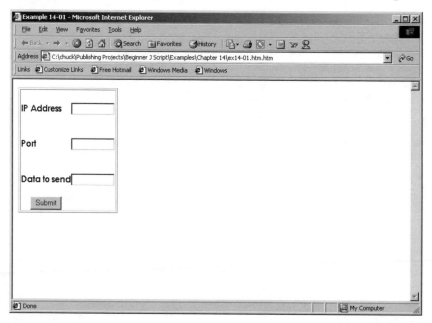

Figure 14-1

This example illustrates using an ActiveX component as a plug-in. The first portion to look at is in the very beginning of the body section of the HTML document.

```
<OBJECT ID="TCPClient"
    CLASSID="CLSID:26900070-7443-11D5-9A47-00409639327E"
    CODEBASE="TCPClientControl.CAB#version=2,0,0,0">
</OBJECT>
```

All ActiveX plug-ins have three properties we are concerned with. The first is the ID. This is simply the name you will use to refer to this plug-in. The second is the classid. A classid is a unique identifier that is created when an ActiveX component is first created. The last property we are concerned with is the codebase property. If a plug-in with the matching classid cannot be found on the client computer, then the location specified in the codebase property will be accessed to install the ActiveX component.

After the ActiveX plug-in is embedded in this fashion we can access any of its properties or methods by simply calling the ID we gave the plug-in followed by a dot ".", then the name of the property or method we wish to access. You see this in the script portion of this example:

```
function send()
{
    var ip
    var port
    var data
    var result

    ip =frmip.ipaddress.value
    port =frmport.port.value
    data =frmdata.data.value

    TCPClient.remoteIP =ip
    TCPClient.remotePort =port
    TCPClient.Message =data

    result =TCPClient.sendData()
    alert(result)
}
```

14

Chapter

## What Plug-ins are Already Installed?

You can use JavaScript to determine if a user has installed a particular plug-in. You can then display embedded plug-in data if the plug-in is installed, or alternative content if it is not. The following example checks for Shockwave and Quicktime plug-ins.

**Example 14-2**

```
<HTML>
<HEAD>
    <TITLE> Example 14-02</TITLE>
</HEAD>
<SCRIPT LANGUAGE="JavaScript">
    var quickplug = navigator.plugins["Quicktime"];
    if (quickplug)
    {
        document.writeln("You already have Quicktime")
    }
    else
    {
        document.writeln("You don't have Quicktime<BR>")
    }

    var shockplug = navigator.plugins["Shockwave"];
    if (shockplug)
        document.writeln("You already have Shockwave")
    else
        document.writeln("You don't have Shockwave")
</SCRIPT><BODY BGCOLOR = white>
</BODY>
</HTML>
```

If you enter the code properly, you will have the status of these plug-ins displayed on a web page. When run on my PC, the following output was generated:

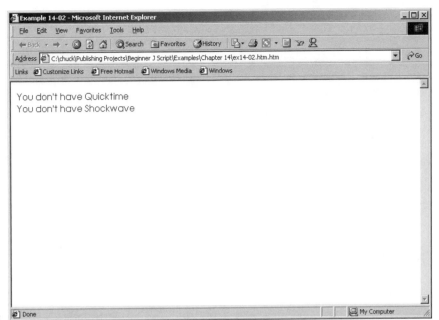

Figure 14-2

# LiveAudio

LiveAudio is used to play a variety of sound files in many formats including WAV, AIFF, AU, and MIDI formats. Audio controls appear according to the size specified in the WIDTH and HEIGHT parameters in the <EMBED> tag. You can create an audio console with any of the following views:

■ console—This gives you a stereo style console with several controls you can use.

■ smallConsole—Consists of a Play, Stop, and volume control lever. The buttons in this view are smaller than those in a console.

■ playButton—A button that starts the sound playing.

■ pauseButton—A button that pauses (without unloading) the sound while it is playing.

■ stopButton—A button that ends the playing of sound and unloads it.

■ volumeLever—A lever that adjusts the volume level for playback of the sound (and adjusts the system's volume level).

Here is the general HTML syntax for a LiveAudio control:

```
<EMBED SRC=[URL] AUTOSTART=[TRUE|FALSE] LOOP=[TRUE|FALSE|INTEGER]
STARTTIME=[MINUTES:SECONDS] ENDTIME=[MINUTES:SECONDS] VOLUME=[0-100]
WIDTH=[#PIXELS] HEIGHT=[#PIXELS] ALIGN=[TOP|BOTTOM|CENTER|BASELINE
|LEFT|RIGHT|TEXTTOP|MIDDLE|ABSMIDDLE|ABSBOTTOM] CONTROLS=[CONSOLE
|SMALLCONSOLE|PLAYBUTTON|PAUSEBUTTON|STOPBUTTON|VOLUMELEVER] HIDDEN=[TRUE]
MASTERSOUND NAME=[UNIQUE NAME TO GROUP CONTROLS TOGETHER SO THAT THEY CONTROL
ONE SOUND]...>
```

The syntax may seem very complicated, but a close look shows that it does not consist of many attributes. What's misleading is that there are many different values that can be given to each attribute. Here is a short description of each attribute and the values it accepts:

SRC=[*URL*]—The URL of the source sound file. If the sound file is stored in the same folder as the HTML document then you can just put the file name with extension.

AUTOSTART=[TRUE|FALSE]—When set to TRUE, the sound will begin playing automatically upon loading the HTML page. The default is FALSE.

LOOP=[TRUE|FALSE|*INTEGER*]—When set to TRUE, the sound will play continuously until the Stop button is clicked on the console or the user goes to another page. If an *INTEGER* value is used, the sound repeats the number of times indicated.

STARTTIME=[*MINUTES:SECONDS*]—Use STARTTIME to specify where the playback should begin. If you want to begin the sound at 30 seconds, you would set the value to 00:30.

ENDTIME=[*MINUTES:SECONDS*]—Use ENDTIME to specify where in the sound file you would like playback to end. If you want to stop the sound at 1.5 minutes, you would set the value to 01:30.

VOLUME=[0-100]—This is a percentage of max volume. The values 1 to 100 are accepted.

WIDTH=[*#PIXELS*]—Use WIDTH to change the width of the console or console element. For CONSOLE and SMALLCONSOLE, the default is WIDTH=144. For VOLUMELEVER, the default is WIDTH=74. For a button, the default is WIDTH=37 (WIDTH=34 looks much better).

HEIGHT=[#*PIXELS*]—Use HEIGHT to change the height of the console. For CONSOLE, the default is HEIGHT=60. For SMALLCONSOLE, the default is HEIGHT=15. For VOLUMELEVER, the default is HEIGHT=20. For a button, the default is HEIGHT=22.

ALIGN=[TOP|BOTTOM|CENTER|BASELINE|LEFT|RIGHT| TEXTTOP|MIDDLE|ABSMIDDLE|ABSBOTTOM]—While RIGHT and LEFT specify the position of the console with respect to the page, the other options tell Netscape Navigator how you want to align text as it flows around the consoles. It acts similarly to the ALIGN attribute of the <IMG> tag. The default value is BOTTOM.

CONTROLS=[CONSOLE|SMALLCONSOLE|PLAYBUTTON|PAUSEBUT TON|STOPBUTTON|VOLUMELEVER]—Use this attribute to select the control you want to place on your page. The default for this field is CONSOLE.

HIDDEN=[TRUE]—The value for this attribute should be TRUE, or it should not be included in the <EMBED> tag. If it is specified as TRUE, no controls will load and the sound will act as a background one.

MASTERSOUND—This value must be used when grouping sounds together in a NAME group. It takes no value (it must merely be present in the <EMBED> tag), but tells LiveAudio which file is a genuine sound file and allows it to ignore any stub files. In order to associate several EMBEDs with one sound file, all EMBEDs should have the same name (see the NAME attribute). The SRC attribute of one of those EMBEDs should be the URL of the actual sound file, whereas the other SRC attributes should specify the URL of a stub file. A stub file is a text file containing a single space (that's the recommended content). Its name should consist of a sound extension (e.g., .mid, .wav, .aif). To create a page with four LiveAudio elements (Play, Pause, Stop, and Volume) all controlling the same file, you need to create three sound stubs and of course have one legitimate sound file (for a total of four EMBEDs). Anytime you use the NAME attribute in a LiveAudio <EMBED>, you must also use a MASTERSOUND attribute. LiveAudio will play no sound when a NAME attribute exists without a corresponding MASTERSOUND attribute, even if that is the only <EMBED> with that name on the page. Since you do not want LiveAudio to attempt to play a stub file (it contains no sound data), you should specify a NAME attribute with no MASTERSOUND attribute. The <EMBED> reflecting the legitimate sound file, on the other hand, should feature MASTERSOUND in order to play.

14

Chapter

NAME=[*UNIQUE NAME*]—This attribute sets a unique ID for a group of EMBEDs (each with a distinct CONTROLS attribute), so they all act on the same sound as it plays. The deficiency of EMBED's syntax is that it takes only one value for CONTROLS. For example, if a content creator wishes to have one sound controlled by two embedded objects (a PLAYBUTTON and a STOPBUTTON), he or she must use two separate EMBEDs and group them by the NAME attribute. In this case, the MASTERSOUND tag is necessary to flag LiveAudio and let it know which of the two <EMBED> tags actually has the sound file you wish to control. LiveAudio ignores any EMBED(s) with no MASTERSOUND tag.

If you want one VOLUMELEVER to control multiple NAMEs (or the system volume), create an EMBED using VOLUMELEVER as the CONTROL. Then set NAME to "_MASTERVOLUME".

The following example illustrates how to do this. To use this sample code, simply substitute any valid .mid file where I have written "sample.mid."

### Example 14-3

```
<HTML>
<HEAD>
<TITLE>Example 14-03</TITLE>
</HEAD>
<BODY>
     <TABLE BORDER=1><TR>
     <TD BGCOLOR="black" ALIGN="center">
     Sample Music
<EMBED SRC="sample.mid"
     AUTOSTART=FALSE
     LOOP=FALSE
     CONTROLS=PLAYBUTTON
     WIDTH=30
     HEIGHT=20
     MASTERSOUND
     NAME="sample1">
<EMBED SRC="stub1.aif"
     AUTOSTART=FALSE
     LOOP=FALSE
     CONTROLS=STOPBUTTON
     WIDTH=34
     HEIGHT=22
     NAME="90210">
<EMBED SRC="stub2.aif"
     AUTOSTART=FALSE
```

```
        LOOP=FALSE
        CONTROLS=PAUSEBUTTON
        WIDTH=34
        HEIGHT=22
        NAME="sample1">
    </TABLE>
    </BODY>
    </HTML>
```

## Antique Bookstore Project

I am not going to add a plug-in to our antique bookstore project because I feel it would simply clutter the web site. However, you should feel free to experiment with the techniques presented in this chapter.

## Summary

In this chapter I showed you the basics of how to add plug-ins to your HTML pages. I think you will find that using plug-ins can add a dimension to your web pages that you cannot attain otherwise.

**14**

Chapter

# Chapter 15

# Objects in JavaScript

Throughout this book I have been using the term "object." By now you have probably gleaned what this means from context. The purpose of this chapter is to provide a little more depth to your understanding of the term.

An *object* is a programming abstraction that groups data with the code that operates on it. All programs contain data of different types. An object simply wraps all that up in a single place, called an object. We did talk about the String object in Chapter 12 and the Math object in Chapter 13. Remember that each held data, but also had methods you could call. A method is just a name for a function that is inside an object.

## Properties

All the objects you can see and touch have characteristics. This book, for example, has width, weight, title, number of pages, etc. These attributes distinguish this book from all other books. These features are called *properties* or *fields* in OO (object-oriented) terminology. An object's property stores data related to the object. Think of properties as adjectives or nouns that will further describe the object.

JavaScript supports two different types of objects:

- *Built-in objects,* such as the String and Math objects
- *User-defined objects*, ones you create

### Using Properties

An object's properties hold its data. You can refer to properties using the following syntax:

```
object.propertyName
```

*object* is the name of the object that the property belongs to. For example, you can assign an object to a variable and then refer to its properties using this variable, followed by the property specification. *propertyName* is the name of the property.

Another important concept is that a property belongs to an object, and only to one object. Think about it this way. The height of this book is just that, the height of <u>this</u> book, and not of some other book.

A dot separates each object from its property. A hierarchical object structure, with objects and properties at different levels, uses the same syntax:

```
object1.object2Property1.object3Property2.property3
```

The following statements demonstrate referencing to elements of a hierarchical object structure:

```
var d = a.b.d
document.write(d) // prints 16
var e = a.b.e
document.write(e) // prints 42
var f = a.c.f
document.write(f) // prints true
var g = a.c.g
document.write(g) // prints king
var h = a.c.h
document.write(h) // prints 13
var i = a.c.i
document.write(i) // prints 10
```

As you can see, a variable may be named exactly like a property of an object. This is possible because properties are not at the same scope as variables, objects, and properties.

## Methods

As you know, objects consist of both data (properties) and functions that handle the data. These functions are called *methods*. Methods enable an object to perform different actions, mostly on its own properties. Think of methods as verbs associated with an object.

JavaScript's implementation of objects is not as powerful as that of Java, so some OO programming advantages that apply to Java do not apply to JavaScript. But remember that you have already used JavaScript objects and you will probably use more. So you should at least be familiar with the terminology.

## Using Methods

A method is called in the following fashion:

```
objectReference.methodName([arguments])
```

*objectReference* is the name of the object, or any other reference. *methodName* is the name of the method, and *arguments* are the arguments that the method accepts.

Because a method is a function, the name of the method is always followed by a pair of parentheses. This rule applies also to methods that do not accept arguments.

You probably find this syntax familiar. I have been using document.write([*expression*]) to print HTML expressions to the page. write() is a method belonging to the built-in document object.

When you create an instance of an object using the new operator, you are really declaring a new data type according to the object's definition and allocating the appropriate amount of memory for that data type. Once you have created an instance of an object, you do not have to use the new keyword anymore when referring to that instance.

# Object-Oriented Concepts

Object-oriented programming is only partially supported in JavaScript. For full support of object orientation you would have to use a programming language such as C++ or Java. With that said, I thought you should at least be introduced to the basic terminology of object orientation. You have already been introduced to properties and functions. These two terms are probably the most important. The next term to remember is instantiation.

JavaScript is based on a scaled-down object-oriented paradigm. This paradigm is often called object based, as opposed to object oriented. In fully object-oriented languages you write classes. A *class* is a template you create for creating objects. Classes do not exist in JavaScript (all objects belong to one "class" that is built into JavaScript). Packages are source files that have one or more related classes. Since classes do not exist in JavaScript, neither do packages.

Many of the more advanced features of object orientation are not supported in JavaScript. For instance, you won't find inheritance (where one class inherits the public methods and properties of another). This is primarily because there are no classes.

There are four concepts that are integral to the entire process of object-oriented programming. They are abstraction, encapsulation, inheritance, and polymorphism.

*Abstraction* is basically the ability to think about concepts in an abstract way. You can create a class for an employee without having to think about a specific employee. It is abstract and can apply to any employee.

*Encapsulation* is really the heart of object-oriented programming. This is simply the act of taking the data and the functions that work on that data and putting them together in a single class. Think back to our coverage of strings and the string class. The string class has the data you need to work on (i.e., the particular string in question) as well as the various functions you might use on that data, all wrapped into one class.

*Inheritance* is a process whereby one class inherits, or gets, the public properties and methods of another class. The classic example is to create a class called "animal." This class has properties such as weight, and methods such as move and eat. All animals would share these same properties and methods. When you wish to create a class for, say a monkey, you then have class monkey inherit from class animal, and it will have the same methods and properties that animal has. This is one way in which object-oriented programming supports code reuse.

*Polymorphism* literally means "many forms." When you inherit the properties and methods of a class, you need not leave them as you find them. You can alter them in your own class. This will allow you to change the form those methods and properties take.

## Building Your Own Objects

Now for the big question, what about building your own objects? We have already used some of JavaScript's built-in objects, such as the String and Date objects. Now you should be ready to learn something about building your own new objects and using them.

## Constructor Functions

All objects have constructor functions. A constructor function is simply a function that defines the properties and methods of the object. It fires automatically when an instance of the object is created. You can think of built-in objects as objects whose constructor functions are predefined in JavaScript.

The this keyword is probably the most important word related to objects in object-oriented programming. It refers to the current object, or instance. If I am sitting in my den and I say "this chair is uncomfortable," it is clear that I am referring to the current room I am in, not some other room. The keyword this is much the same. You can create many instances of an object. The this keyword allows you to specify the current instance the code is running in. Inside a constructor function it refers to the instance for which the function was called. Take a look at the following function:

```
function student(name, age, avgGrade)
{
    this.name = name
    this.age = age
    this.grade = avgGrade
}
```

This function accepts three arguments. It defines an object type of a student in a class. The properties are name, age, and grade, and they are initialized by the values passed on to the function. You can use the following statement to create an instance of this object—a student in a class:

```
var student1 = new student("Sharon", 16, 85)
```

Now you can refer to these properties in the following fashion:

```
alert(student1.name + " is a cute " + student1.age + " - year old.)
```

It is also possible to add properties to an object once it has been created. Such properties exist only in the specific instance to which they are assigned. The following script segment demonstrates this:

```
function student(name, age, avgGrade)
{
    this.name = name
    this.age = age
    this.grade = avgGrade
}
var student1 = new student("Sharon", 16, 85)
student1.sex = "female"
```

**15**

Chapter

```
var message = student1.name + " is a cute " + student1.age
message += " - year old "
message += (student1.sex == "female") ? "girl." : "boy."
alert(message)
```

Now that we have these concepts down, let me show them in action.

Based on the exact definition of the word this, some JavaScript tends to use alternative structures for construction functions. Here is the preceding example in a different form:

```
function student(name, age, avgGrade, sex)
{
    obj = this
    obj.name = name
    obj.age = age
    obj.grade = avgGrade
    obj.description = (sex == "female") ? "girl" : "boy"
}
```

## Summary

I freely admit that this topic may be quite difficult for beginning programmers. Some of you may choose to skip it for now. It is included in this book merely to get you started.

In this chapter I discussed the basics of object-oriented terminology and concepts. I also discussed how those concepts are implemented in JavaScript, and which ones are not. You can certainly write scripts without any knowledge of object orientation, but hopefully this information will give you a deeper understanding of what is occurring in your scripts.

# Chapter 16

# Tips and Tricks

This chapter shows you a few interesting tips and tricks. Some of these are JavaScript tricks, and some are HTML tricks. It is quite difficult to completely separate HTML from JavaScript, since JavaScript runs inside of HTML documents. These tips and tricks are placed here because they either did not fit into the topic content of one of the preceding chapters or seem a little bit advanced for this book. In either case I hope that you find these scripts to be useful for you.

## Inline Frames

The latest versions of both Internet Explorer and Netscape support a new tag called <IFRAME>. Let's take a look at how this tag works in an actual web page.

**Example 16-1**

```
<HTML>
<HEAD>
     <TITLE>Example 16-01</TITLE>
</HEAD>
<BODY>
     <IFRAME WIDTH = 400 HEIGHT = 250 SRC = "frame.htm" >
     </IFRAME>
</BODY>
</HTML>
```

This literally displays one HTML document inside another. If you enter all the code properly, or use the sample in the code files, you should be able to view this in your browser and see something like this:

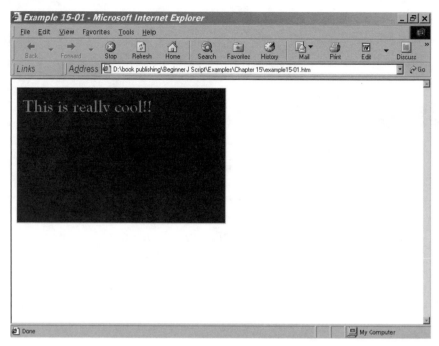

Figure 16-1

One of the cool effects you can create with the new <IFRAME> tag is that you can make the inline frame transparent. Add ALLOWTRANSPARENCY= "true" to the <IFRAME> element tag. Then add STYLE="background-color:transparent" to the <BODY> tag of <fileName> that is being sourced in the <IFRAME> tag (SRC=<fileName>).

The following code will implement this:

```
<IFRAME NAME="Frame1" SRC="somepage.htm"
ALLOWTRANSPARENCY="true" STYLE="position:absolute; top:25; left:50; z-index:3">
```

And the <BODY> tag of somepage.html is:

```
<BODY STYLE="background-color:transparent">
```

The latest versions of both Netscape and Internet Explorer also support inline floating frames. Use the <IFRAME> tag to specify the NAME of the frame and its source. Here is the <IFRAME> tag definition:

```
<IFRAME NAME="Frame1" SRC="somepage.htm">
</IFRAME>
```

# Browser Detection

While it is true that browsers are available as free downloads, it is also true that not everyone always downloads the latest to their machine. So it is possible that someone might be using an older browser when viewing your page, and that might mean that their browser does not support all the JavaScript you are using. For that reason, adding some browser detection might be in order. Here is the code:

```
var IE4 = (document.all && !document.getElementById) ? true : false;
var IE5 = (document.all && document.getElementById) ? true : false;
var NET4 = (document.layers) ? true : false;
var NET6 = (document.getElementById && !document.all) ? true : false;
```

Now you can tell which browser is being used by checking each of the variables to see if it is true. Only one will show true, and that will be the browser currently in use.

# System Information

JavaScript can retrieve a significant amount of information about the drives in your system, both disk drives as well as shared networks. A drive object is created using the GetDrive() method of the FileSystemObject object. Here is an example:

```
GetDrive(letterDrive);
```

The single parameter, letterDrive, is the given drive name. This method returns the drive object. The following script would create a drive object for c:

```
<SCRIPT LANGUAGE="JavaScript">
var fso = new ActiveXObject("Scripting.FileSystemObject");
driveObj = fso.GetDrive("c");
</SCRIPT>
```

The drive object does not have any methods, but it does have some very useful properties:

| Property | Description |
|---|---|
| AvailableSpace | Returns the number of free bytes on the given drive |
| DriveLetter | Returns the drive letter of a physical local drive or a shared network |
| DriveType | Returns the drive type |
| FileSystem | Returns the file system type for the specified drive |

**16**

Chapter

| Property | Description |
|----------|-------------|
| FreeSpace | Returns the number of free bytes on the given drive |
| IsReady | Returns the status of the drive |
| Path | Returns the path of the given drive |
| RootFolder | Returns the folder object of the root folder |
| SerialNumber | Returns the unique serial number of the volume |
| ShareName | Returns the shared name of a network drive |
| TotalSize | Returns the total size, in bytes, of a specified drive |
| VolumeName | Sets or returns the volume name of the specified drive |

If you have experience with Windows programming you might notice that this works a lot like the Windows FileSystemObject provided by scrun.dll (used frequently by Visual Basic and Visual C++ developers).

## Finding Mouse Location

Here is an interesting little piece of JavaScript code that will find out where the exact x and y coordinates of the mouse click event are. For this sample I display those coordinates but you could use this code to do particular actions depending on the mouse position.

```
document.onclick = printEvent;
function printEvent(e)
{
    if (navigator.appName == "Netscape")
    {
        mm_X = e.pageX;
        m_Y = e.pageY;

    }
    else
    {
        m_X = event.clientX;
        m_Y = event.clientY;
    }
  alert("The Mouse click  was at x  coordinate= " + m_X + " and y
            coordinate = " + m_Y);
}
```

## Password

Often you will want someone to enter in a username and password, and you will then use your JavaScript to log them into the web site. It is very useful to have the password masked. On most software, when you enter a password, asterisks (*) are what actually appear on the screen. Fortunately, this is easy to do by simply changing one simple tag in your HTML form code.

You may have used something like this to allow the user to enter a username and password:

```
<FORM NAME ="frmname">

     Username <INPUT TYPE="text" NAME = "name" VALUE="" SIZE=10>
     <BR>
     Password <INPUT TYPE="text" NAME ="password" VALUE=""
SIZE=10>

</FORM>
```

Simply change the INPUT TYPE from "text" to "password" and it will give you the desired effect.

```
<FORM NAME ="frmname">

     Username <INPUT TYPE="text" NAME = "name" VALUE="" SIZE=10>
     <BR>
     Password <INPUT TYPE="password" NAME ="password" VALUE=""
SIZE=10>

</FORM>
```

**16**

Chapter

## Browser Information

Sometimes it is useful to be able to detect things about a user's browser. Some of this was covered in previous chapters. However, here is a simple script that will give you the user's screen resolution, browser type, and version number.

**Example 16-2**

```
<HTML>
<HEAD>
<TITLE> Example 16-02</TITLE>
```

```
<SCRIPT LANGUAGE= "JavaScript">


    var sheight = screen.height
    var swidth = screen.width
    var browsername = navigator.appname
    var version =navigator.appVersion
    alert("Your screen resolution is " + sheight + " X " + swidth)
    alert("You are using " + browsername + " version " + version)

</SCRIPT>

</HEAD>

<BODY BGCOLOR=White>
</BODY>
</HTML>
```

# Printing the Page

This little script will allow your users to click a single button and print the current page. This can be quite useful and I recommend you use it frequently.

**Example 16-3**

```
<HTML>
<HEAD>
<TITLE>Example 16-03</TITLE>
</HEAD>
<BODY BGCOLOR=White>
<INPUT TYPE="submit" name="print" value="Print"onclick="window.print()">
</BODY>
</HTML>
```

# Antique Bookstore Project

As with most of the chapters in this book, this chapter will add to our antique bookstore project. In this case we are simply going to add a Print button to one inventory screen (you could add a button to all of them if you so desired). We will add it to the completeinventory.htm page.

```
<HTML>
<HEAD>
<TITLE>Complete Inventory</TITLE>
```

```
<SCRIPT LANGUAGE="JAVASCRIPT">

function toggleMenu(currMenu)
{
    if (document.getElementById)
    {
        thisMenu = document.getElementById(currMenu).style
        if (thisMenu.display == "block")
        {
            thisMenu.display = "none"
        }
        else
            {
                thisMenu.display = "block"
            }
            return false
        }
        else
        {
            return true
        }
}

</SCRIPT>
<STYLE TYPE="TEXT/CSS">
   .menu   {display:none; margin-left:20px}
</STYLE>
</HEAD>
<BODY background="back1.gif">

<H3>
    <A HREF="completeinventory.htm"onClick="return toggleMenu('menu1')">Books
            from the 1800's</A>
</H3>
<SPAN CLASS="menu" ID="menu1">
    1st Edition Charles Dickens' "Tale of Two Cities"<BR>
    1st Edition Edgar Allen Poe's "The Tell-Tale Heart"<BR>
    Signed Copy of Edgar Allen Poe's "The Cask of Amontillado"<BR>

</SPAN>
<H3>
    <A HREF="completeinventory.htm" onClick="return toggleMenu('menu2')">Books
            from the 1700's</A>
</H3>
<SPAN CLASS="menu" ID="menu2">
    Ben Franklin's memoirs<BR>
```

```
        "How to Start a Revolution"<BR>
        "Political Theory" by Thomas Paine
</SPAN>
<H3>
        <A HREF="completeinventory.htm" onClick="return toggleMenu('menu3')">Books
                for under $25</A>
</H3>
<SPAN CLASS="menu" ID="menu3">
    A cowboy's diary (circa 1850's)<BR>
    4th edition Charles Dickens' "A Tale of Two Cities"
    3rd Edition Jules Verne's "20,000 Leagues Under the Sea"
</SPAN>

<H3>
        <A HREF="completeinventory.htm" onClick="return toggleMenu('menu4')">Our
                finest items</A>
</H3>
<SPAN CLASS="menu" ID="menu4">
    Signed copy of Shakespeare's "Hamlet"<BR>
    Gutenberg's diary<BR>
    Signed first Edition Longfellow
    1570 Hebrew Bible
</SPAN>

<CENTER><input type="submit" name="print" value="Print"onclick="window.print()">
</CENTER>
</BODY>
</HTML>
```

## View the Directory

This next script is rather short but very useful. It allows you to view the current directory in your browser in a Windows Explorer format. You can then browse the entire hard drive via your browser.

**Example 16-4**

```
<HTML>
<HEAD>
<TITLE>Example 16-04</TITLE>
</HEAD>
<SCRIPT LANGUAGE="JavaScript">

function getListing()
{
    var url = location.href
```

```
        var lastSlash = url.lastIndexOf("/")
        location.href = url.substring(0, lastSlash + 1)
    }

    </SCRIPT>
    <BODY>
    <FORM>
    <INPUT TYPE="button" VALUE=" view directory listing " onClick="getListing()">
    </FORM>
    </BODY>
    </HTML>
```

If you entered the code properly, you should be able to see something like this.

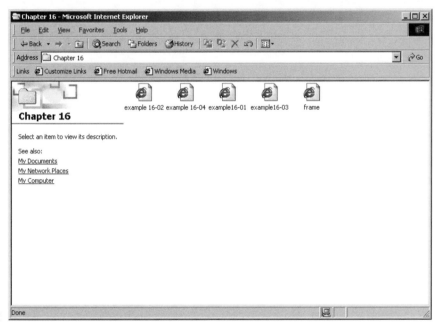

Figure 16-2

## Summary

This chapter simply listed a few interesting tricks you can do in JavaScript. I strongly suggest that you visit the web sites listed in Appendix A. These web sites have hundreds of free scripts you can download, tutorials, and much more. While most of this book has focused on teaching you specific techniques you can use in JavaScript, this chapter's purpose has been to introduce you to a few techniques that did not seem to fit into the other chapters.

16

Chapter

# Chapter 17

# JavaScript Games

They say that all work and no fun makes Jack a dull boy. Well, this chapter is about fun! Here I am going to show you a few relatively simple games done all in JavaScript. These games will use the techniques you have already learned, but will use then in novel ways. I think you will find this to be a very exciting chapter.

## Press the Button

Let's start with a rather simple example. In this game you simply place a button on the screen and ask the user to press it. However, when they try to press it, you move it, and change its message.

**Example 17-1**

```
<HTML>
<HEAD>
<TITLE>Example 17-01</title>
<SCRIPT LANGUAGE="JavaScript">
init_msg="PRESS BUTTON NOW"
function new_msg()
{
    var msg=new Array()

    msg[0]="I said press the button"
    msg[1]="Come on, press the button"
    msg[2]="You can't even press a simple button?"
    msg[3]="Use your mouse!"
    msg[4]="Left-click your mouse on the button!"
    var num1=parseInt(Math.random()*(width-150))
    var num2=parseInt(Math.random()*(height-150))
    var num3=parseInt(Math.random()*msg.length)
    ActualObj.left=num1
    ActualObj.top=num2
```

```
        document.clickme.button.value=msg[num3]
}

function start()
{
    if(document.all)
    {
        ActualObj=eval(document.all.floatLyr.style);
        width=document.body.clientWidth
        height=document.body.clientHeight
    }
    else if(document.layers)
    {
        ActualObj=eval(document.floatLyr.document)
        width=innerWidth
        height=innerHeight
    }
    document.clickme.button.value=init_msg
    ActualObj.backgroundColor=document.bgColor
}

function caught()
{
    alert("You caught me!")
}

</SCRIPT>
</HEAD>
<BODY onload="start()" bgcolor="white">
<CENTER>Please press the button</center>
<div onmouseover="new_msg()" id="floatLyr"
style="position:absolute;visibility:visible;top:40;left:40">
<FORM name="clickme">
    <TABLE width="100" border="1" bordercolor=White cellspacing="0"
            bgcolor=White>

    <tr>
        <td>
            <INPUT name="button" onmouseover="new_msg()"
                onmousedown="caught()" type="Button" onkeypress="caught()">

</TABLE>
</FORM>
</DIV>
</BODY>
</HTML>
```

If you entered the code properly you should now be able to see a screen that looks like this:

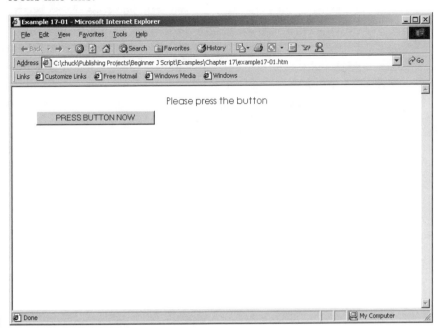

Figure 17-1

When you try to move your mouse over the button it will move, like this:

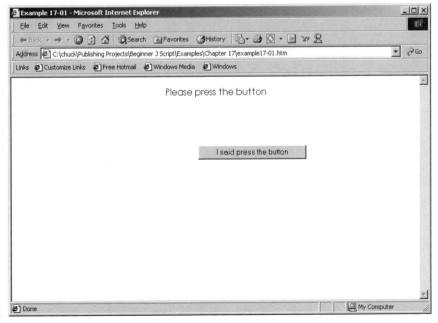

Figure 17-2

# Roll the Dice

There are many games that require random dice rolls. Most board games utilize six-sided dice, whereas many role-playing games utilize various multisided dice. Whatever your needs, this script will generate random dice rolls for you, with any type of dice you wish. You can also easily modify this to accommodate more dice or more types of dice.

**Example 17-2**

```
<HTML>
<HEAD>
<SCRIPT LANGUAGE = "JavaScript">
     var die = 6    // Default dice type
     var dice = 1  // default number of dice
     function rolldice(die, dice)
     {
          var roll = 0
          for (I=0; I< dice; I++)
     {
          roll = roll + Math.round(Math.random() * die) % die + 1;
     }
     document.form.text.value = roll
     }
</SCRIPT>
<BODY>
<CENTER>
<FORM name=form>
     <TABLE border=1 bgcolor = gray>
          <tr>
               <td>What kind of dice do you want to roll?
               <td>How many?
          <tr>
               <td>
                    <P><INPUT TYPE=radio name=sides onclick="die = 3">3 Sided
                    <P><INPUT TYPE=radio name=sides onclick="die = 4">4 Sided
                    <P><INPUT TYPE=radio name=sides onclick="die = 5">5 Sided
                    <P><INPUT TYPE=radio checked name=sides onclick="die =
                         6">6 Sided
                    <P><INPUT TYPE=radio name=sides onclick="die = 8">8 Sided
               <td>
                    <P><INPUT TYPE=radio name=sides onclick="die = 10">10 Sided
                    <P><INPUT TYPE=radio name=sides onclick="die = 12">12 Sided
                    <P><INPUT TYPE=radio name=sides onclick="die = 20">20 Sided
                    <P><INPUT TYPE=radio name=sides onclick="die = 30">30 Sided
```

```
                    <P><INPUT TYPE=radio name=sides onclick="die =
                        100">100 Sided
            <td>
                <P><INPUT TYPE=radio name=number onclick="dice = 1">1
                <P><INPUT TYPE=radio name=number onclick="dice = 2">2
                <P><INPUT TYPE=radio name=number onclick="dice = 3">3
                <P><INPUT TYPE=radio name=number onclick="dice = 4">4
                <P><INPUT TYPE=radio name=number onclick="dice = 5">5
            <td>
                <P><INPUT TYPE=radio name=number onclick="dice = 6">6
                <P><INPUT TYPE=radio name=number onclick="dice = 7">7
                <P><INPUT TYPE=radio name=number onclick="dice = 8">8
                <P><INPUT TYPE=radio name=number onclick="dice = 9">9
                <P><INPUT TYPE=radio name=number onclick="dice = 10">10
        <tr>
            <td>
                <INPUT TYPE=button value="Roll Dice" name=button
                        onclick="rolldice(die, dice)">
                <INPUT TYPE=text size=10 name=text>
        </TABLE>
    </FORM>
    </CENTER>
    </BODY>
    </HTML>
```

If you entered the code properly, you should be able to view something like the following figure:

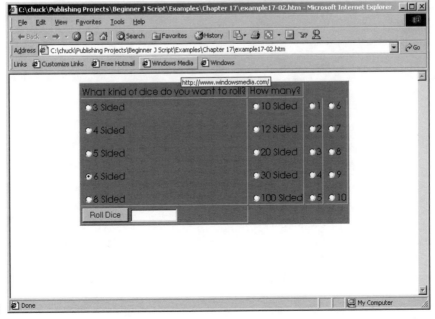

Figure 17-3

# Viva Las Vegas

This next example is a blackjack game that is fairly simple. The techniques are all ones that you have used previously in this book. They are simply combined in such a way as to give you a working blackjack game.

**Example 17-3**

```
<HTML>
<HEAD>
<TITLE> Example 17-03</TITLE>
<SCRIPT LANGUAGE="JavaScript">
     var gameOver
     var cardCount
     function Shuffle(max)
     {
          var num=Math.random()*max
          return Math.round(num)+1
     }
     function getSuit()
     {
          suit = Shuffle(4)
          if(suit == 1)
               return "Spades"

          if(suit == 2)
               return "Clubs"

          if(suit == 3)
               return "Diamonds"

          else
               return "Hearts"
     }

function cardName(card)
{
    if(card == 1)
         return "Ace"

    if(card == 11)
         return "Jack"

    if(card == 12)
         return "Queen"
```

```
        if(card == 13)
            return "King"

    return "" + card
}

function cardValue(card,strWho)
{
    if(card == 1)
    {
        if(strWho =="You" && document.display.you.value >10)
        {
            document.display.say2.value=document.display.say2.value+" Low"
            return 1
        }
        else
            return 11
    }

    if(card > 10)
        return 10

return card
}

function PickACard(strWho)
{
    card = Shuffle(12)
    suit = getSuit()

    if(strWho =="You")
        document.display.say2.value=(cardName(card) + " of " + suit)

    else
        document.display.say1.value=(cardName(card) + " of " + suit)

    return cardValue(card,strWho)
}

function NewHand(form)
{
    if(gameOver !=0)
    {
        form.say1.value=("Hand in Play!")
        form.say2.value=("")
        return
```

**17**

Chapter

```
        }
        else
        {
            form.dealer.value = 0
            form.you.value = 0
            cardCount=0
            form.dealer.value = eval(form.dealer.value) + PickACard("Dealer")
            form.you.value = eval(form.you.value) + PickACard("You")
            gameOver = -1
            cardCount+=1
        }
    }

    function Dealer(form)
    {
        if (gameOver ==0)
        {
            form.say1.value=("Please Deal the Cards")
            form.say2.value=("")
            return
        }

        if (cardCount <2)
        {
            form.say1.value=("There is a Minimum of 2 Cards")
            form.say2.value=("Hit Again")
            return
        }
        else
        {
            while(form.dealer.value < 17)
            {
                form.dealer.value = eval(form.dealer.value) + PickACard("Dealer")
            }
        }

    }

    function User(form)
    {
        if (gameOver ==0)
        {
            form.say1.value=("Please Deal the Cards")
            form.say2.value=(" ")
            return
        }
```

```
    else
    {
        cardCount+=1
        form.say1.value="You Get...."
        form.you.value = eval(form.you.value) + PickACard("You")
    }

    if(form.you.value > 21)
    {
        form.say1.value=("Sorry, you lose")
        gameOver=0
        form.numgames.value=(eval(form.numgames.value)) -1
    }
}

function LookAtHands(form)
{
    if (gameOver ==0 || form.you.value<10 || cardCount <2)
    {
        return
    }

    else
        if(form.dealer.value > 21)
        {
            form.say1.value=("Dealer loses")
            form.say2.value=("You Win")
            gameOver=0
            form.numgames.value=(eval(form.numgames.value))+1
        }

    else
    if(form.you.value > form.dealer.value)
    {
        form.say1.value=("You Win")
        form.say2.value=(" ")
        gameOver=0
        form.numgames.value=eval(form.numgames.value)+1
    }
    else
    {
        if(form.dealer.value == form.you.value)
        {
            form.say1.value=("Game Tied!")
            form.say2.value=("Try Again!")
```

```
                gameOver=0
                form.numgames.value=eval(form.numgames.value)-1
            }
            else
            {
                form.say1.value=("House Wins!")
                form.say2.value=("Tough Luck!")
                gameOver=0
                form.numgames.value=eval(form.numgames.value)-1
            }
        }
    }
}
function initialize()
{
    gameOver=0
    cardCount=0;
    document.display.dealer.value=""
    document.display.you.value=""
    document.display.numgames.value="0"
    document.display.say1.value=" Press the Deal button"
    document.display.say2.value="To Start!"
}

</SCRIPT>

<BODY OnLoad="initialize()">

<CENTER>
    <FORM NAME="display">
        <TABLE BGCOLOR=GRAY border="1">
        <TR>
            <TD><CENTER>Score:</CENTER>
            <TD><CENTER>Dealer</CENTER>
            <TD><CENTER><INPUT TYPE=text name="dealer" size="2"></CENTER>
            <TD><CENTER>Card(s):  <INPUT TYPE=text name="say1"
                    value=""></CENTER>

        <TR>
            <TD><CENTER><INPUT TYPE=text name="numgames"value="0"></CENTER>
            <TD><CENTER>Player</CENTER>
            <TD><CENTER><INPUT TYPE=text name="you"></CENTER>
            <TD><CENTER>Card(s):  <INPUT TYPE=text name="say2"value="">
                    </CENTER>
```

```
<TR>
    <TD><CENTER><INPUT TYPE=button value="Deal"
            onClick="NewHand(this.form)"></CENTER>
    <TD><CENTER><INPUT TYPE=button value="Stand"
            onClick="Dealer(this.form);LookAtHands(this.form);">
    <INPUT TYPE=button value=" Hit " onClick="User(this.form)">
            </CENTER>
    </TABLE>
</FORM>
</CENTER>

</BODY>
</HTML>
```

If you enter all the code properly, you should be able to see something like the following figure.

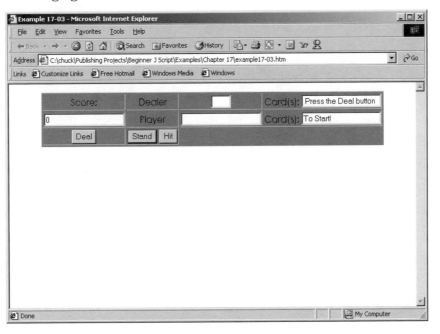

Figure 17-4

## Summary

This chapter was placed in this book simply to show you some fun things you can do with JavaScript. As you are working to learn the technical nuances of any programming or scripting language, it is important that you go beyond simply memorizing syntax. With a little bit of imagination, you can take basic techniques and produce truly creative results. Albert Einstein once said that "imagination is greater than knowledge." Well, most of this book was concerned with increasing your knowledge; hopefully, this chapter sparked your imagination.

# Chapter 18

# ActiveX and JavaScript

JavaScript is probably the most widely used technology for enhancing web pages. However, there are other popular technologies being used as well. In an earlier chapter I introduced you to cascading style sheets. In this chapter I will introduce you to ActiveX components. These can only be used in Microsoft Internet Explorer.

## Theoretical Background

Before we delve into the use of ActiveX components, let's take a look at some of the theory underlying them. A frequent problem in programming is allowing two different components to communicate. One popular technology that makes this possible is COM (Component Object Model). With COM, it does not matter what programming language a component is written in as long as it has an interface that conforms to COM standards. The two most common programming tools used to create COM components are Microsoft Visual C++ and Microsoft Visual Basic.

ActiveX is a technology based on COM. All ActiveX components adhere to COM interface specifications. The two most common implementations of ActiveX components are ActiveX controls and ActiveX DLLs. ActiveX controls are quite familiar to Visual Basic programmers. They are also commonly seen on web sites. If you go to a web site that wishes to download a component to your hard drive, chances are it's an ActiveX control. These are commonly used with playing multimedia. An ActiveX control usually has a visible interface.

ActiveX DLLs expose a number of functions that the host applications (or web page) can use. However, ActiveX DLLs rarely have a user interface. ActiveX controls are far more common in web pages than ActiveX DLLs.

# Using ActiveX for TCP/IP

Let's look at an actual example of using an ActiveX component in a web page with Java Script. In the Chapter 18 folder in the code files you will find an ActiveX control named TCPClientControl.ocx. This is a control I developed to allow easy access to TCP/IP communication inside of web pages. It is very simple to use, and you should feel free to use this control as you wish.

The first step in using an ActiveX control is simply inserting it in the web page. This was covered briefly in Chapter 14, "Adding Plug-ins." The code to insert an ActiveX component into a web page is really rather simple:

```
<OBJECT ID="TCPClient"
    CLASSID="CLSID:26900070-7443-11D5-9A47-00409639327E"
    CODEBASE="TCPClientControl.CAB#version=2,0,0,0">
</OBJECT>
```

The <OBJECT> tag is an HTML tag identifying that an ActiveX component is being inserted. OBJECT ID is simply the name you wish to use for this component within your code. You can choose any name you wish. Once you have chosen a name you can use that name to access the methods and properties of the ActiveX component. CLASSID is a unique number that each ActiveX component has. It is generated when the ActiveX component is created. CODEBASE identifies the URL from which the ActiveX component can be downloaded if it is not already installed on the user's computer. This is an especially nice feature of ActiveX components: they are self-installing.

The method I have just explained to you is the same for all ActiveX components. Now I will show you an actual example of an ActiveX control in use. This example creates an ActiveX TCP/IP client that can send data to any active TCP/IP server on the Internet.

**Example 18-1**

```
<HTML>
<HEAD>
    <TITLE>Example 18-01</TITLE>
<SCRIPT LANGUAGE = "JavaScript">
function send()
{
    var ip
    var port
    var message
```

```
        ip = frmdestination.remoteip.value
        port = frmdestination.remoteport.value
        message = frmdestination.message.value

        TCPClient.remoteIP = ip
        TCPClient.remotePort =port
        TCPClient.Message =message
        TCPClient.sendData()
    }
    </SCRIPT>
    </HEAD>
    <BODY>
    <P>
    <CENTER>
        <TABLE BORDER = 1 BGCOLOR = lightblue>
        <TR>
            <TD>
                <FORM name ="frmdestination">
                    IP Address<INPUT TYPE="text" NAME ="remoteip" VALUE=""
                        SIZE=15><BR>
                    Port Number<INPUT TYPE="text" NAME ="remoteport" VALUE=""
                        SIZE=15><BR>
                    Message<INPUT TYPE="text" NAME ="message" VALUE=""
                        SIZE=25><BR>
                    <INPUT TYPE ="button" VALUE ="Connect" onClick="send()">
                </FORM>
        </TABLE>
    </CENTER>
    <OBJECT ID="TCPClient"
        CLASSID="CLSID:26900070-7443-11D5-9A47-00409639327E"
        CODEBASE="TCPClientControl.CAB#version=2,0,0,0">
    </OBJECT>
    </BODY>
    </HTML>
```

If you entered all the code properly you will be able to see the following:

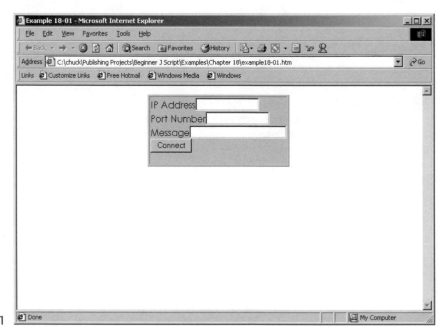

Figure 18-1

This example shows you an easy way to utilize ActiveX controls in your web site. In this case the ActiveX control takes care of the TCP/IP communication with some TCP/IP server.

## Ticking Clock

This next little component offers a nice visual effect. It places a clock anywhere you wish on your web page. This is a rather easy method for inserting a clock on your web page.

### Example 18-2

```
<HTML>
<HEAD>
    <TITLE>Example 18-02</TITLE>
<SCRIPT LANGUAGE = "JavaScript">
</SCRIPT>
</HEAD>
<BODY>
<CENTER>
    <OBJECT ID="Active_Clock"
        CLASSID="CLSID:A119E782-3E4F-4EF8-A959-FA3FD028076E"
        CODEBASE="ActiveClock.CAB#version=1,0,0,0">
    </OBJECT>
```

```
</CENTER>
</BODY>
</HTML>
```

If you enter the code properly, you should be able to view this web page in Internet Explorer and see the following image.

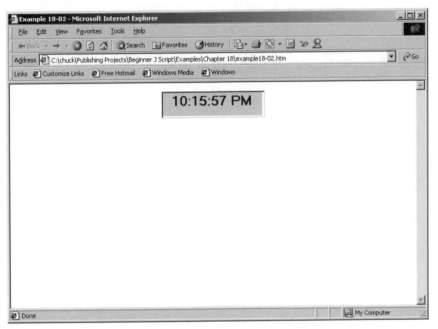

Figure 18-2

## Slider Text

This ActiveX component is interesting for several reasons. First of all, I am interested in it because I use it frequently to teach students how to create their own ActiveX components. It is also interesting for us because with this ActiveX component, I can show you how to manipulate an ActiveX component's properties via JavaScript. Most ActiveX components come with some documentation telling you what properties and methods they have and what they do.

**Example 18-3**

```
<HTML>
<HEAD>
      <TITLE>Example 18-03</TITLE>

<SCRIPT LANGUAGE = "JavaScript">
      function setslider()
```

18

Chapter

```
            {
                SliderText.Max = 50
                SliderText.flagextreme =true
            }
        </SCRIPT>
        </HEAD>
        <BODY onLoad = "setslider()">
        <CENTER>
        <OBJECT ID="SliderText"
                CLASSID="CLSID:1E0822BF-195D-11D5-9A46-00409639327E"
                CODEBASE="slidertext1.CAB#version=1,0,0,0">
        </OBJECT>
        </CENTER>
        </BODY>
        </HTML>
```

If you entered all the code properly, you will be able to see this image:

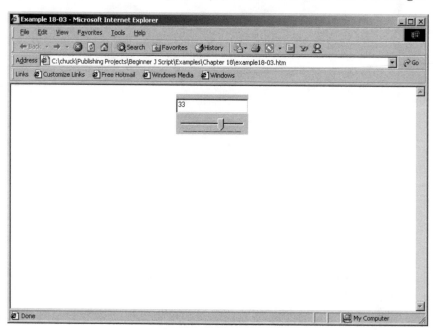

Figure 18-3

## Summary

This chapter is not meant to be an exhaustive treatment of the topic of ActiveX. However, I hope that after reading this chapter you will realize that ActiveX components are one more tool you have at your disposal for creating truly stunning web sites. Often ActiveX is used in conjunction with VB Script; however, now you should realize that it is really not very hard to use it with JavaScript as well. I also hope you realize that taking advantage of existing ActiveX components can allow you to greatly expand your web sites.

**18**

Chapter

# Chapter 19

# Programming and JavaScript

This book has focused on accomplishing specific goals using JavaScript. This chapter is included to introduce you to some concepts that are common to programming. Certainly a person simply using JavaScript for their own personal web page should feel free to skip this chapter. However, a professional web developer needs to understand what programming is, how it's done, and how it relates to JavaScript. This chapter also lays the groundwork for those of you who wish to continue on to my *Advanced JavaScript, Second Edition* book (also available from Wordware Publishing).

## General Concepts

We have used variables throughout this book, but what exactly are they? A *variable* is a place in memory set aside to hold data. The variable's name allows us to refer to that place in memory and to manipulate the data held therein. Without variables you would have to refer to the actual hexadecimal address in memory where data is stored. In many languages, data is stored in variables of a specific type. Whole numbers are stored in integer data types, decimals are stored in float data types, etc. In JavaScript the var keyword allows you to declare a variable that will hold any type of data. This is very convenient for you when you are writing scripts.

A *statement* is a line of code that performs some action. The following are statements:

```
var mydate    // the action performed is the declaration of a variable
var mynumber = x * 3  // The action performed is a mathematical operation.
```

When you group statements together into a logical grouping under some name, you have a *function*. A function may or may not take any parameters, and may or may not return some value. In other programming languages you have to define the function in such a way as to have it return data of a specific

**217**

type. In JavaScript you have the freedom to return any type of data you wish, or to return no data at all.

Now that we have defined variables, statements, and functions, we have defined the foundations of all programming. Combining this with a knowledge of operators (introduced to you in Chapter 13, "Math in JavaScript") and you have the basic building blocks of programming. The primary difference between scripting languages, like JavaScript, and traditional programming languages, such as C and Java, is that scripting languages are much more flexible. You can do things any way you please. However, this can frequently lead to code that is very difficult to read and maintain.

Good coding practices are really quite simple. The first thing to keep in mind is to make your code readable. You will notice that I space my code out. It is quite possible to place more than one statement on a single line, but I avoid that because it does not facilitate readable code. The next thing I highly recommend is the liberal use of comments. Comments can make your code more understandable. Simply place a // and anything written after it will be ignored by the browser. This way you can leave explanatory comments telling the reader what you are doing in your code.

## Arrays

*Arrays* are data structures, and are somewhat more complex than simple variables. When you have related data that you wish to group together, an array provides a very good way to do that. An example would be a set of student grades. If you want to process an individual item of an array you need to specify the array name and indicate which array element is being referenced. Specific elements are indicated by an index or a subscript.

Arrays in JavaScript are simple built-in objects. You create an array just like an instance of an object, because that is exactly what it is. The formal name of the object is Array—notice the capitalized "A." The general syntax is:

```
var arrayObjectName = new Array()
var arrayObjectName = new Array(arrayLength)
```

*arrayObjectName* is the name of a new object, an existing variable, or a property of an existing object.

*ArrayLength* is the number of individual elements in the array.

In JavaScript you do not have to specify the actual size of the array, nor the type of variables it will contain. This is because JavaScript will allow you to expand the array if needed, and you can place in any type of data you wish.

Here are some arrays:

```
var day = new Array(31)
var month = new Array(12)
var year = new Array() // number of years "not known"
```

All elements of an array are initially null. This is important because such elements do not have any influence on your script. An element with a null value actually does not exist. This is why it is common practice to give each element of an array an initial value. As you might guess, this is referred to as *initializing* an array.

From the moment an array is declared, it takes up the required storage area in memory.

It also does not matter if you initialized its values or not. Theoretically, if you created an array without specifying the number of elements, it would be as if you created one with zero elements.

To use an array you must be able to refer to its elements. Arrays in JavaScript are objects. Like all other objects, they have properties and methods:

```
arrayObjectName[subscript] // ar1[4]
```

The *subscript* follows the array name and is enclosed in square brackets. Subscripts are simple integers that start at zero.

Here is a simple array:

```
var ar = new Array(5)
```

This array has five elements: ar[0], ar[1], ar[2], ar[3], ar[4].

After you create an array you can increase its length by specifying a value for the highest subscript element. The following code creates an array of length zero, then assigns a null value to element 99. This changes the length of the array to 100.

```
accounts = new Array()   // array of zero elements
accounts[99] = null      // array of 100 elements
```

Note that the array does not take up any storage space, even after it is extended.

When referring to an element, the subscript can be either a literal (e.g., 3) or a variable (e.g., num = 3).

An element of an array can be any valid value. It can be a string, a number, a Boolean value, a null value, or even another object. For example, if you want to create an array in which each element is a student object, you can use the following statements:

```
function student()
{    // constructor function
     // properties not initialized to meaningful value
     this.name = ""
     this.age = ""
     this.grade = ""
}
var size = 35                       // num of students in class
var students = new Array(size)      // array is defined
for (var i = 0; i < size; i++)
{
     students[i] = new student()
}
students[0].name = "Mark"
students[32].grade = 88
```

At first, the desired size of the array—the number of students in the class—is assigned to the variable size. An array of that size is then created. All elements of the array, from students[0] to students[34], are then defined using the constructor function student(). In this example, all of the elements in the array are of the same type. An array can also have elements of different types. Here is an example:

```
function student()
{    // constructor function
     // properties not initialized to meaningful value
     this.name = ""
     this.age = ""
     this.grade = ""
}
function teacher(name, age)
{
     this.name = name
     this.age = age
}
var size = 35                            // num of students in class
var students = new Array(size + 1)  // array is defined
students[0] = new teacher("Kate", 45)
```

```
for (var i = 1; i < size + 1; i++)
{ // or i <= size
    students[i] = new student()
}

alert("   is the teacher." + students[0].name)
```

In this script segment an array of size + 1 elements is defined, because the first element, students[0], holds an instance of the teacher object.

The most important rule is that the subscript, or index, starts at zero. Although it might seem quite awkward, use this element like all other elements of the array.

## Summary

The purpose of this chapter was to introduce you to concepts common to all types of programming. This knowledge is not necessary for the hobbyist but is vital for the professional programmer (or the would-be professional). If you wish to explore these concepts in more depth, as well as exploring JavaScript in greater depth, may I humbly recommend my own *Advanced JavaScript, Second Edition* from Wordware Publishing.

# Chapter 20

# Antique Bookstore Project

Throughout most of this book we have gradually been building a real-world web site for a fictitious antique bookstore. This chapter simply brings all the source code into one convenient location. You can also find that same code in the Antique Bookstore Project folder in the code files.

## The Main Screen

First I will show you the main screen, which contains index.htm, main.htm, banner.htm, and tool.htm. Main.htm has the frame code to hold the other pages.

*index.htm*

```
<HTML>
<HEAD>
<TITLE>Ye Olde Book Shoppe</TITLE>
</HEAD>
<FRAMESET rows="64,*">
    <FRAME name="banner" scrolling="no" noresize target="contents"
                src="banner.htm">
    <FRAMESET cols="169,*">
        <FRAME name="contents" target="main" src="tool.htm" scrolling="auto">
        <FRAME name="display" src="main.htm" scrolling="auto" target="_self"
                marginwidth="0" marginheight="16">
    </FRAMESET>
    <NOFRAMES>
    <BODY>

    <P>This page uses frames, but your browser doesn't support them.</P>

    </BODY>
    </NOFRAMES>
</FRAMESET>
```

```
</HTML>
```

*main.htm*

```
<HTML>
<HEAD>
    <TITLE>Ye Olde Book Shoppe</TITLE>
<SCRIPT LANGUAGE="JavaScript">

function setCookie(name, value, expires, path, domain, secure)
{
    var curCookie = name + "=" + escape(value) +
        ((expires) ? "; expires=" + expires.toGMTString() : "") +
    ((path) ? "; path=" + path : "") +
    ((domain) ? "; domain=" + domain : "") +
    ((secure) ? "; secure" : "")
    document.cookie = curCookie
}


function getCookie(name)
{
var prefix = name + "="
    var cookieStartIndex = document.cookie.indexOf(prefix)

        if (cookieStartIndex == -1)
        return null

        var cookieEndIndex = document.cookie.indexOf(";", cookieStartIndex+
                prefix.length)

        if (cookieEndIndex == -1)
        cookieEndIndex = document.cookie.length

        return unescape(document.cookie.substring(cookieStartIndex
                +prefix.length, cookieEndIndex))
}

function deleteCookie(name, path, domain)
{
    if (getCookie(name))
    {
        document.cookie = name + "=" +((path) ? "; path=" + path : "") +
                ((domain) ? "; domain=" + domain : "") +"; expires=Thu,
                01-Jan-70 00:00:01 GMT"
    }
}
```

```
        var expiredate= new Date()
        expiredate.setTime(expiredate.getTime() + 30 * 24 * 60 * 60 * 1000)
        var name = getCookie("name")
        if (!name)
        {
            name = prompt("Please enter your name:", "John Doe")
            setCookie("name", name, expiredate)
        }
alert("Welcome back " + name)
</SCRIPT>
<SCRIPT LANGUAGE="JavaScript">
var mydate = new Date()
var myday = mydate.getDay()
if(myday==0)
    alert("Sunday- Sorry, we are closed today")
if (myday==1)
    alert("Monday- Sorry, we are closed today")

if(myday==2)
    alert("Tuesday- Our hours today are 10 a.m. to 6 p.m.")

if(myday==3)
    alert("Wednesday- Our hours today are 10 a.m. to 6 p.m.")

if (myday==4)
    alert("Thursday- Our hours today are 10 a.m. to 6 p.m.")

if (myday==5)
    alert("Friday- Our hours today are 10 a.m. to 7 p.m.")

if (myday==6)
    alert("Saturday- Our hours today are 10 a.m. to 4 p.m.")

</SCRIPT>
    <SCRIPT LANGUAGE="JAVASCRIPT">
        ImageArray = new Array("banner1.gif","banner2.gif","banner3.gif")
        CurrentImage = 0
        ImageCount = ImageArray.length
        function RotateBanner()
        {
            if (document.images)
            {
                CurrentImage++
                if (CurrentImage ==ImageCount)
                {
                    CurrentImage = 0
```

20

Chapter

```
                    }
                    document.Banner.src=ImageArray[CurrentImage]
                            setTimeout("RotateBanner()",3000)
            }
        }


</SCRIPT>
</HEAD>
<BODY  background="back1.gif"  onLoad="RotateBanner()">
<SCRIPT LANGUAGE="JavaScript">
    var bgOffset = 0;
    var bgObject = eval('document.body');

    function scrollbackground(maxSize)
    {
        bgOffset = bgOffset + 1;

        if (bgOffset > maxSize)
            bgOffset = 0;

        bgObject.style.backgroundPosition = "0 " + bgOffset;
    }
var scrtimer = window.setInterval("scrollbackground(50)",50);

</SCRIPT>
<CENTER>
<IMG SRC="banner1.gif"  NAME="Banner" >
<P><TABLE BORDER=1>
    <TR>
        <TD>
            <P><IMG SRC="gargshelf.gif">
        <TD>
            <P><CENTER>Ye Olde Book Shoppe</CENTER>
        <TD>
            <IMG SRC="gargshelf.gif">

</TABLE>

<P>
<P>


</CENTER>
<P>
</BODY>
```

```
</HTML>

tool.htm

<HTML>
<HEAD>
     <TITLE>Ye Olde Book Shoppe</TITLE>
</HEAD>
<BODY background="back1.gif">
<P>
     <A HREF = "books.htm" target = "display">See our books</A><BR>
     <A HREF = "inventory.htm" target = "display">Latest Additions</A><BR>
     <A HREF = "completeinventory.htm" target = "display">Complete
                Inventory</A><BR>
     <A HREF = "compute.htm" target = "display">Compute Costs</A><BR>
</BODY>
</HTML>

banner.htm

<HTML>
<HEAD>
     <TITLE>Ye Olde Book Shoppe</TITLE>
</HEAD>
<BODY background="sample1.gif">
<CENTER>
<H1><B><I>Ye Olde Booke Shoppe</I> </B></H1>
</CENTER>
</BODY>
</HTML>
```

These pages you have just seen make up the primary portions of the web site.
This is what the user will see when they first visit the web site. Now let's look
at the inventory pages.

# Inventory Pages

```
inventory.htm

<HTML>
<HEAD>
     <TITLE>Book Inventory</TITLE>

<SCRIPT LANGUAGE="JAVASCRIPT" >

     var childwindow = null

     function openbook1()
```

```
        {
            childwindow = window.open("inventory1.htm","childwindow",
                    "width=400,height=400,scrollbars=yes")
        }
        function openbook2()
        {
            childwindow = window.open("inventory2.htm","childwindow",
                    "width=400,height=400,scrollbars=yes")
        }
        function openbook3()
        {
            childwindow = window.open("inventory3.htm","childwindow",
                    "width=400,height=400,scrollbars=yes")
        }
        function openbook4()
        {
            childwindow = window.open("inventory4.htm","childwindow",
                    "width=400,height=400,scrollbars=yes")
        }
</SCRIPT
</HEAD>
<BODY   background="back1.gif" >
<P>
<CENTER>
        <H2> This month's newest additions!
</CENTER>
        <P>
        <A HREF="javascript:openbook1()"
        onMouseOver= " window.status='We have three copies of this book, all
                in fine condition'
        return true" onMouseOut="window.status= ' '
        return true">View Shakespeare</A><BR>

        <A HREF="javascript:openbook2()"
        onMouseOver= " window.status='We just acquired this book last month'
        return true" onMouseOut="window.status= ' '
        return true">View Dickens</A><BR>

        <A HREF="javascript:openbook3()"
        onMouseOver= " window.status='This book is in fair condition'
        return true" onMouseOut="window.status= ' '
        return true">View Poe</A><BR>

        <A HREF="javascript:openbook4()"
        onMouseOver= " window.status='We have one copy in mint condition'
        return true" onMouseOut="window.status= ' '
```

```
            return true">View King James Bible</A><BR>
            </H2>

</BODY>
</HTML>
```

*inventory1.htm*

```
<HTML>
<HEAD>
     <TITLE>Advanced JavaScript</TITLE>
</HEAD>
<BODY BACKGROUND ="bod-bg.gif">
<BR>
<BR>
<CENTER>
     <IMG SRC = "book1.gif" Height = 100 Width = 100>
           <BR>
           <BR>
           Signed copy of "Macbeth"
           $2900
</CENTER>
</BODY>
</HTML>
```

*inventory2.htm*

```
<HTML>
<HEAD>
     <TITLE>Advanced JavaScript</TITLE>
</HEAD>
<BODY BACKGROUND ="bod-bg.gif">
<BR>
<BR>
<CENTER>
     <IMG SRC = "book2.gif" Height = 100 Width = 100>
           <BR>
           <BR>
           Mint condition first edition "A Tale of Two Cities"
           $1200
</CENTER>
</BODY>
</HTML>
```

*inventory3.htm*

```
<HTML>
<HEAD>
     <TITLE>Advanced JavaScript</TITLE>
```

```
</HEAD>
<BODY BACKGROUND ="bod-bg.gif">
<BR>
<BR>
<CENTER>
    <IMG SRC = "book3.gif" Height = 100 Width = 100>
        <BR>
        <BR>
        Signed First Edition of "The Raven"
        $1450
</CENTER>
</BODY>
</HTML>
```

*inventory4.htm*

```
<HTML>
<HEAD>
    <TITLE>Advanced JavaScript</TITLE>
</HEAD>
<BODY BACKGROUND ="bod-bg.gif">
<BR>
<BR>
<CENTER>
    <IMG SRC = "book4.gif" Height = 100 Width = 100>
        <BR>
        <BR>
        The original King James Bible
        $10450
</CENTER>
</BODY>
</HTML>
```

*complete inventory.htm*

```
<HTML>
<HEAD>
<TITLE>Complete Inventory</TITLE>
<SCRIPT LANGUAGE="JAVASCRIPT">

function toggleMenu(currMenu)
{
    if (document.getElementById)
    {
        thisMenu = document.getElementById(currMenu).style
        if (thisMenu.display == "block")
        {
            thisMenu.display = "none"
```

```
            }
            else
            {
                 thisMenu.display = "block"
            }
            return false
        }
        else
        {
            return true
        }
    }

</SCRIPT>
<STYLE TYPE="TEXT/CSS">
    .menu   {display:none; margin-left:20px}
</STYLE>
</HEAD>
<BODY background="back1.gif">

<H3>
    <A HREF="completeinventory.htm"onClick="return toggleMenu('menu1')">Books
            from the 1800s</A>
</H3>
<SPAN CLASS="menu" ID="menu1">
    1st Edition Charles Dickens' "A Tale of Two Cities"<BR>
    1st Edition Edgar Allen Poe's "The Tell-Tale Heart"<BR>
    Signed Copy of Edgar Allen Poe's "The Cask of Amontillado"<BR>

</SPAN>
<H3>
    <A HREF="completeinventory.htm" onClick="return toggleMenu('menu2')">Books
            from the 1700's</A>
</H3>
<SPAN CLASS="menu" ID="menu2">
    Ben Franklin's memoirs<BR>
    "How to Start a Revolution"<BR>
    "Political Theory" by Thomas Paine
</SPAN>
<H3>
    <A HREF="completeinventory.htm" onClick="return toggleMenu('menu3')">Books
            for under $25</A>
</H3>
<SPAN CLASS="menu" ID="menu3">
    A Cowboy's diary (circa 1850's)<BR>
    4th edition Charles Dickens' "A Tale of Two Cities"
```

```
        3rd Edition Jules Verne's "20,000 Leagues Under the Sea"
    </SPAN>

    <H3>
        <A HREF="completeinventory.htm" onClick="return toggleMenu('menu4')">Our
                finest items</A>
    </H3>
    <SPAN CLASS="menu" ID="menu4">
        Signed copy of Shakespeare's "Hamlet"<BR>
        Gutenberg's diary<BR>
        Signed first Edition Longfellow
        1570 Hebrew Bible
    </SPAN>

    <CENTER><input type="submit" name="print" value="Print"onclick="window.print()">
    </CENTER>
    </BODY>
    </HTML>
```

# Finishing the Pages

Now for the final two pages. The books.htm page gives us the ability to flip through the books that are currently being showcased. Compute.htm gives us the ability to compute costs.

*books.htm*

```
<HTML>
<HEAD>
    <TITLE>Book Inventory</TITLE>
<SCRIPT LANGUAGE="JAVASCRIPT" >
    PicArray = new Array("book1.gif","book2.gif","book3.gif","book4.gif")
    CurrentPic = 0
    ImageCount = PicArray.length - 1

    function MovePrevious()
    {
        if (document.images && CurrentPic > 0)
        {
        CurrentPic--
            document.myPicture.src=PicArray[CurrentPic]
        }
    }

    function MoveNext()
    {
```

```
            if (document.images && CurrentPic < ImageCount )
            {
                CurrentPic++
                document.myPicture.src=PicArray[CurrentPic]
            }
        }


    </SCRIPT>
</HEAD>
<BODY background="back1.gif" >
<P>
<CENTER>
        <H2>This month's specials!</H2>
    <IMG SRC="book1.gif" HEIGHT=300 WIDTH =300 NAME="myPicture" ALT="Our
            Book Inventory">
    <FORM>
        <INPUT TYPE="button" VALUE="<--" onClick="MovePrevious()">
        <INPUT TYPE ="button" VALUE ="-->" onClick="MoveNext()">
    </FORM>
</CENTER>
</BODY>
</HTML>
```

*compute.htm*

```
<HTML>
<HEAD>
    <TITLE>Computer Costs</TITLE>
<SCRIPT LANGUAGE="JAVASCRIPT" >
    function total()
    {
        var shipping
        var tax
        var total

        var numbooks = txtbooks.value
        var price = txtprice.value

        tax = price * .0875
        shipping = numbooks * 1.5
        total = eval(price) + eval(tax) + eval(shipping)

        txttax.value = tax
        txtship.value = shipping
        txttotal.value = total
    }
```

```
        </SCRIPT>
        </HEAD>
        <BODY    background="back1.gif" >
        <P>
        <CENTER>
        <TABLE BORDER = 1>
            <TR>
                <TD>
                    Number of books ordered <INPUT TYPE=text NAME="txtbooks"
                            VALUE=""><BR>
                    Total price of books ordered<INPUT TYPE = text NAME = "txtprice"
                            VALUE = ""><BR>
                    <INPUT TYPE=button NAME="Submit" VALUE="Compute"
                            onclick="total()">

            <TR>
                <TD>
                    <INPUT TYPE=text NAME="txttax" VALUE=""> Tax<BR>
                    <INPUT TYPE=text NAME="txtship" VALUE="">Shipping Costs <BR>
                    <INPUT TYPE=text NAME="txttotal" VALUE=""> Total<BR>
        </TABLE>
        </CENTER>
        </BODY>
        </HTML>
```

# Summary

The purpose of this chapter is bring together all of the work you have been doing. Here in one place is the complete source code for the entire antique bookstore project. All the required images are included in the code files. It is my sincere wish that you have learned a lot while working your way through this book.

# Online Resources

Below I have compiled a list of what I consider to be the best JavaScript sites on the web. You can consult these sites in order to get tutorials, source code, and much more. I strongly recommend that you familiarize yourself with these web sites.

## JavaScript Web Sites

JavaScript.com is one of the premier JavaScript sites. It has hundreds of tutorials and samples. You'll really want to use this one.
http://www.javascript.com/

Doc JavaScript is another excellent site you would do well to reference.
http://www.webreference.com/js/

A1 JavaScript is a site with some interesting source code you might wish to review.
http://www.a1javascripts.com/

JavaScript Gate is a pretty solid site with lots of source code and tutorials.
http://javascriptgate.com/

JavaScript World is, as the name implies, a compilation of hundreds of tutorials and source code.
http://webdeveloper.com/

JavaScript Games is a page with a number of games written in JavaScript. It's a good page to look at to see what you can do with JavaScript.
http://plaza.harmonix.ne.jp/~jimmeans/

## HTML Web Sites

HTML Reference is a good site with a reference to HTML 4.0 as well as JavaScript and other scripting languages.
http://www.geocities.com/pbb_webref/

The official HTML 4.0 Specification is an excellent resource to find out exactly what is included in HTML 4.0.
http://www.w3.org/TR/REC-html40/

## Organizational Web Sites

HTML Writers Guild is an association of HTML writers.
http://www.hwg.org/

International WebMasters Association is an association of web masters and developers. They have a variety of interesting membership benefits.
http://www.irwa.org/

## Image Collections

When you are creating web sites, you need access to lots of images. The following sites are my favorites:

The Animation Factory at http://www.animfactory.com has a wonderful collection of animated gifs.

Gifs That Don't Suck at http://spitfire.cwv.net/~cdbailey/ is the place to find odd animations. You have to check this site out!

## Certification Web Sites

If you are looking to prove that you have learned JavaScript, BrainBench has a JavaScript certification test you can take online:
http://www.brainbench.com

# Employment Web Sites

If you are seeking employment, there are a couple of web sites you should check out:

Computer Jobs.com http://www.computerjobs.com

Jobs for Programmers http://www.prgjobs.com

# HTML Reference

This is not meant to be a comprehensive HTML reference. It is simply a reference for the essential HTML tags that you must know in order to construct web pages.

## Basic HTML Structure

<HTML> </HTML> Defines an HTML document.

<HEAD> </HEAD> Defines the header section.

<TITLE> </TITLE> Defines the title that appears in the browser.

<BODY> </BODY> Defines the body of the HTML document.

<SCRIPT LANGUAGE="JavaScript"> </SCRIPT> Defines a JavaScript.

## Body Formatting Tags

<BODY BGCOLOR=blue> Sets the web page's background color.

<BODY BACKGROUND="mypic.jpg"> Sets the background of the page to an image.

<BODY BGCOLOR=white TEXT=black LINK=blue VLINK=red ALINK=green> Sets the background color, text color, link color, visited link color, and active link color for the web page.

## Images

To insert an image in your page you merely need to add the following:

<IMG SRC="mypic.gif">

**239**

## Links

Text that is a web page link:

<A HREF="http://www.wordware.com"> link to Wordware Publishing</A>

An image that is a web page link:

<A HREF="http://www.wordware.com"> <IMG SRC="some picture.gif"</A>

Text that is an e-mail link:

<A HREF="mailto:chuckeasttom@yahoo.com"> email me!</A>

An image that is an e-mail link:

<A HREF="mailto:chuckeasttom@yahoo.com"><IMG SRC="somepic.gif"></A>

## Lists

Unordered list:

<UL>
   <LI> Item one
   <LI>Item two
</UL>

Ordered list:

<OL TYPE= I>
   <LI>
   <LI>
</OL>

## Marquee

<MARQUEE BGCOLOR = yellow ALIGN Center LOOP=infinite>
This is a scrolling marquee.
</MARQUEE>

## Tables

```
<TABLE BORDER =1>
  <TR>
    <TD> Row one cell 1
    <TD> Row one cell 2
  <TR>
    <TD> Row two cell 1
    <TD> Row two cell 2
</TABLE>
```

You can also set the background color of the table, a single row, or even a single cell:

```
<TABLE BORDER=1 BGCOLOR=Blue>
```

```
<TR BGCOLOR=yellow>
```

```
<TD BGCOLOR=green>
```

## Text Formatting Tags

Italics <I> *this is italics* </I>

Bold <B> **this is bold** </B>

Underline <U> this is underlined</U>

Setting font <FONT FACE="Arial"> this is Arial font </FONT>

<BR> this is a line break

<P> new paragraph

## Form Tags

<FORM> </FORM> Defines an HTML form.

<INPUT TYPE=text NAME="txttest" VALUE="Enter Text Here"> This defines a text field named txttest with an initial value of Enter Text Here.

<INPUT TYPE=button NAME="Submit" VALUE="OK" > This defines a button named Submit that has a caption of OK.

# JavaScript Reference

*abs* Returns the absolute (unsigned) value of its argument. Abs is a method of Math.

```
document.write(Math.abs(−5));
document.write(Math.abs(5))
```

These examples both return 5.

*acos* Returns the arc cosine (0 to pi radians) of its argument. The argument must be a number between −1 and 1. If the value is outside this range, a zero is returned. Method of Math. Also see asin, atan, cos, sin, tan.

*alert* Displays a JavaScript Alert dialog box with an OK button and a user-defined message. See also METHODS confirm and prompt.

*alinkColor* The color of a link after the mouse button is depressed—but before it's released—and expressed as a hexadecimal RGB triplet or string literal.

*appCodeName* Returns a read-only string with the code name of the browser.

*appName* Returns a read-only string with the name of the browser. See also appCodeName, appVersion.

*appVersion* Returns a string with the version information of the browser.

```
document.write(navigator.appVersion)
```

returns

```
6.0 (Win95)
```

This specifies Navigator 6.0 running on Windows 95 with an international release. See also appName, appCodeName.

*asin* Returns the arc sine (between –pi/2 and pi/2 radians) of a number between –1 and 1. If the number is outside this range, a zero is returned. Method of Math. See also acos, atan, cos, sin, tan.

*atan* Returns the arc tangent (between –pi/2 and pi/2 radians) of a number between –1 and 1. If the number is outside this range, a zero is returned. Method of Math. See also acos, asin, cos, sin, tan.

*back* Recalls the previous URL from the history list. This method is the same as history.go(–1). Method of the history object. See also forward and go.

*bgColor* The document background color expressed as a hexadecimal number or string literal. Property of document. See also alinkColor, fgColor, linkColor, vlinkColor.

```
document.bgColor = "yellow"
```

*blur* Removes focus from the specified form element. For example, the following line removes focus from feedback:

```
sometext.blur()
```

assuming that feedback is defined as:

```
<input type="text" name="sometext">
```

See also focus and select.

*bold* Formats a string object in bold text by encasing it with HTML <B> tags. Method of string. See also italics, strike.

*ceil* Returns the smallest integer greater than, or equal to, its argument. Method of Math. See also floor.

```
Math.ceil(3.05)
```

returns a 4.

*charAt* Returns the character from a string at the specified index. The first character is at position zero and the last at length –1. Method of string.

```
var userName = "Chuck Easttom"
document.write(userName.charAt(4)
```

returns a "K."

See also indexOf and lastIndexOf.

*checked* A Boolean value (true or false) indicating whether a check box or radio button is selected. The value is updated immediately when an item is checked. Property of checkbox and radio.

*clear* Clears the contents of a window, regardless of how the window was filled. Method of document. See also close, open, write, writeln.

*close* Closes the current window. As with all window commands, the window object is assumed.

```
window.close()
close()
```

both close the current window.

See also clear, open, write, writeln.

*confirm* Displays a JavaScript confirmation dialog box with a message and buttons for OK and Cancel. Confirm returns true if the user selects OK and false for Cancel.

See also alert and prompt.

*cookie* String value of a small piece of information stored in a client-side file. The value stored in the cookie is found using substring charAt, IndexOf, and lastIndexOf.

*cos* Returns the cosine of the argument. The angle must be in radians. Method of Math. See also acos, asin, atan, sin, tan.

*fgColor* The color of foreground text represented as a hexadecimal RGB triplet or a string literal. This value cannot be changed after a document is loaded. Property of document.

See also alinkColor, bgColor, linkColor, vlinkColor.

*floor* Returns the integer less than or equal to its argument. Method of Math.

```
Math.floor(5.78)
```

returns a 5.

See also ceil.

*focus* Navigates to a specific form element and gives it focus.

*fontcolor* Formats the string object to a specific color expressed as a hexadecimal RGB triplet or a string literal, similar to using <font color=*color*>. Method of string.

*fontsize* Formats the string object to a specific font size: one of the seven defined sizes using an integer through the <fontsize=*size*> tag.

*forward* Loads the next document on the URL history list. This method is the same as history.go(1). Method of history. See also back and go.

*getDate* Returns the day of the month as an integer between 1 and 31. Method of Date. See also setDate.

*getDay* Returns the day of the week as an integer from zero (Sunday) to six (Saturday). Method of Date.

*getHours* Returns the hour of the day in 24-hour format, from zero (midnight) to 23 (11 PM). Method of Date. See also setHours.

*getMinutes* Returns the minutes with an integer from zero to 59. Method of Date. See also setMinutes.

*getMonth* Returns the month of the year as an integer between 0 (January) and 11 (December). Method of Date. See also setMonth.

*getSeconds* Returns the seconds in an integer from 0 to 59. Method of Date. See also setSeconds.

*getYear* Returns the year of the date object. Method of Date. See also setYear.

*go* Loads a document specified in the history list by its URL or relative to the current position on the list. If the URL is incomplete, the closest match is used. Method of history. See also back and forward.

*indexOf* Returns the location of a specific character or string, starting the search from a specific location. The first character of the string is specified as zero and the last is the string's length–1. Method of string. See also charAt and lastIndexof.

*italics* Formats a string object into italics by encasing it an HTML <I> tag. Method of string. See also bold, strike.

*lastIndexOf* Returns the index of a character or string in a string object by looking backward from the end of the string or a user-specified index. Method of string. See also charAt and indexOf.

*linkColor* The hyperlink color displayed in the document, expressed as a hexadecimal RGB triplet or as a string literal. It works like the link attribute in the HTML <body> tag. Property of document. See also alinkColor, bgColor, fgColor, vlinkColor.

*open* For a document, opens a stream to collect the output of write or writeln methods. If a document already exists in the target window, then the open method clears it.

*pow* Returns a base raised to an exponent. Method of Math.

*prompt* Displays a prompt dialog box that accepts user input. If an initial value is not specified for inputDefault, the dialog box displays the value <undefined>. Method of window. See also alert and confirm.

*referrer* Returns a read-only URL of the document that called the current document. It can be used to keep track of how users are linked to a page.

```
document.write("You came here from a page at " + document.referrer)
```

*round* Returns the value of a floating-point argument rounded to the next highest integer if the decimal portion is greater than, or equal to, .5, or the next lowest integer is less than .5. Method of Math.

*setDate* Sets the day of the month. Method of Date. See also getDate.

*setHours* Sets the hour for the current time. Method of Date. See also getHours.

*setMinutes* Sets the minutes for the current time. Method of Date. See also getMinutes.

*setMonth* Sets the month with an integer from 0 (January) to 11 (December). Method of Date. See also getMonth.

*setSeconds* Sets the seconds for the current time. Method of Date. See also getSeconds.

*setTime* Sets the value of a date object. Method of Date. See also getTime.

*setYear* Sets the year in the current date. See also getYear.

*sin* Returns the sine of an argument. The argument is the size of an angle expressed in radians, and the returned value is from –1 to 1. Method of Math. See also acos, asin, atan, cos, tan.

*sqrt* Returns the square root of a positive numeric expression. If the argument's value is negative, the returned value is zero.

*tan* Returns the tangent of an argument. The argument is the size of an angle expressed in radians. Method of Math. See also acos, asin, atan, cos, sin.

*toLowerCase* Converts all characters in a string to lowercase. Method of string. See also toUpperCase.

*toUpperCase* Converts all characters in a string to uppercase. Method of string. See also toLowerCase.

*vlinkColor* Returns or sets the color of visited links.

*write* Writes one or more lines to a document window, and can include HTML tags and JavaScript expressions, including numeric, string, and logical values. The write method does not add a new line (<br> or /n) character to the end of the output. Method of document.

*writeln* Writes one or more lines to a document window followed by a new line character.

# Common Errors

Obviously there are a lot of possible errors you could get in your code. My goal in this appendix is to illustrate for you those errors that I find to be the most common. Hopefully if you will begin checking for these errors, your debugging process will be much quicker.

| Error | Example | Solution |
|-------|---------|----------|
| **Spelling** | Var myage<br><br>Myag = 33 | Always double-check your spelling |
| **Missing Brackets** | `<SCRIPT LANGUAGE = "JavaScript">`<br>`Function squarenum()`<br>`{`<br>`    answer = num * num`<br><br>`</SCRIPT>`<br><br>Note: If you don't close the bracket, the browser will try to read the rest of the text as part of your function. | Always make sure that any bracket you open, you also close. |
| **Closing Tags** | `<A HREF=http://wordware.com>`<br>`WordWare publishing`<br><br>Note: Since I omitted the `</A>`, the browser will attempt to execute the rest of the text as part of the hypertext reference. | Many tags need to be closed. Make sure you close all tags that require closing. |

# Index

**251**

# Looking for more?

**Check out Wordware's market-leading Web Programming/Development Library featuring the following new releases and upcoming titles.**

## Available Now!

**Advanced JavaScript 2nd Edition**

1-55622-852-X
$54.95
7½ x 9¼
736 pp.

**Search Engine Positioning**

1-55622-804-X
$49.95
7½ x 9¼
576 pp.

## Coming Soon:

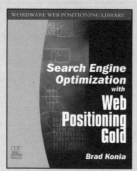

**Search Engine Optimization with Web Positioning Gold**

1-55622-873-2
$36.95
7½ x 9¼
400 pp.

**Delphi Internet Developer's Guide**

1-55622-801-5
$59.95
7½ x 9¼
600 pp.

**The Official Guide to Miva Merchant 4.X**

1-55622-923-2
$42.95
7½ x 9¼
350 pp.

**The Official Guide to Miva Script Programming**

1-55622-872-4
$59.95
7½ x 9¼
400 pp.

**For more information, visit us online at www.wordware.com.**